THE CENTRAL SCHOOL OF SPEECH AND DRAM

UNIVERSITY OF LONDON

Handmade
in
London

By the same author:

Discover Unexpected London

Andrew Lawson

Handmade
in
London

Cassell
London

CASSELL LTD.
35 Red Lion Square, London WC1R 4SG
and at Sydney, Auckland, Toronto, Johannesburg,
an affiliate of
Macmillan Publishing Co., Inc.,
New York.

First published 1978

All photographs by the author

ISBN 0 304 29743 7

Photoset and printed in Great Britain by
Lowe & Brydone Printers Limited, Thetford, Norfolk

F378

To Harold Pound, with admiration

CONTENTS

ACKNOWLEDGEMENTS

First and foremost my warmest thanks to the many craftsmen who have helped me with this book. Some of them are named in the book, but many are not, and I am most grateful to them all. They have taken time from their work to demonstrate and explain, and their enthusiasm has often been a great encouragement in my work on this book. I hope that their generosity to me will not lay them open to further interruptions from more people like me.

Michael Murray of the Clerkenwell Green Association gave me help and advice. Susan Hare, Librarian of the Goldsmiths' Company, was most helpful with information. Bob Gilding kindly allowed me to quote from his book *The Journeyman Coopers of East London*. Ronnie and Jean Goodchild lent me a room with a view to write in. My wife Briony typed until the early hours. And Mary Griffith edited with such self-effacing thoroughness that it will be surprising if this sentence is allowed to stand. To them all, my sincere thanks.

PART I

Craftsmen in London

All over London there are people who earn their living by making things with their hands. The census of 1971 included no fewer than 16,900 'unclassified' craftsmen in the Greater London area. Hidden within this impersonal statistic are individuals like the teapot-handle maker of Hackney, the vellum-maker of Brentford and the candle-maker of Battersea. But the figure does not include the 24,980 tailors, the 57,810 woodworkers and the 4,140 silversmiths who are classified separately.

These multitudes of craftsmen are scattered around London, in High Streets and in quiet back roads, in the centre of the City as well as in the suburbs. Some of them work on their own and improvise workshops from sheds, warehouses, attics and garages. Others work for firms of various sizes, in purpose-built factories and studios.

This silent army of craftsmen remains largely unknown and uncelebrated. They tend to be individualists who seek no publicity and seldom get together to promote a common cause. Their work is often not signed or credited to them, and any praise or honour that it wins is generally given to the firms that employ them, or to the shops that retail the objects that they have made.

Anonymous they may be, but collectively the craftsmen of London make a priceless contribution to the texture and variety of the city's life. Generations of unnamed craftsmen have enriched the decorations and contents of London's finest buildings. Today's Londoners do not have to go far to have their furniture specially built, their books individually bound, their shoes and hats made to measure, their saddles, boats and even cameras made to their own specification. Visitors come to London from all over the world for the same services. Still 'Savile Row' is synonymous with the world's best tailoring, just as 'London Best' is a term used universally to describe the ultimate in fine craftsmanship.

Why London? It seems surprising that this changing city can have remained the crafts capital of England, as it has done for seven hundred years. It is strange that essentially rural crafts such as saddle-making and chair-making should flourish in the heart of a large city when they have died out in so many country districts. One reason is that London is the capital of patronage. The Royal family, Government, the City institutions, the Services, the Church—all have strong roots in London, and they have been the traditional patrons of craftsmen's work. And London's quality shops provide a focus for patronage from abroad.

Many large cities came to specialize in particular industries at the time of the Industrial Revolution, but London kept its rich mix of different trades alive. A wide range of skills have been practised in the City since the Middle Ages, when each craftsman came to be represented by a guild for his particular trade, known as a City Livery Company. The City Companies saw that standards were kept high, and many of them grew wealthy on the success and fortunes of the craftsmen and traders that they represented. Although the influence of the Companies has been much reduced, some of them continue to use their wealth and influence to foster their trades. And

3

the long-established tradition of quality hand-work has survived, so that London remains a centre for small industry.

There are as many interpretations of the word 'craft' as there are skills that come under its banner. In the workshops the word is seldom heard. Men engaged in the craft trades call themselves 'tradesmen' and speak of 'skills of the trade' and so on.

Craft is about skill. It is about the skilful use of tools and the sensitive use of materials. The craftsman comes to be so familiar with his tools that they become extensions of his own body, used instinctively, quickly, gracefully, like his own hands. The true craftsman respects his materials. He brings out the best in them, and his best work emphasizes their beauty. But the word 'craft' can be used in a disparaging sense too, to imply hollow cleverness. 'Crafty' describes a piece of craftwork where skill has become an end in itself. Mere sleight of hand produces slickness. A slick piece of craftsmanship seems to lack purpose, and signifies a craftsman who is not true to his materials, and who lacks conviction about the function or the beauty of the object that he is making.

A pair of shoes or a wooden beer cask are intended by their makers to serve particular functions. And yet, function apart, there is a peculiar beauty in these objects when they are well made. But call the shoemaker or the cooper an artist and he might well feel insulted. Nevertheless there is a necessary element of art in any successful craft work. Good design can be the result of making something in the simplest possible way. Beauty can be born out of the pleasure that the craftsman takes in his materials and the skill with which he shows them to their best advantage. William Morris expressed it in this way: 'Beauty in art is a direct outcome of the workman's pleasure in his work.'

The relationship between art and craft, then, is a blurred one, and it is made all the more confusing by the widely used expression 'artist-craftsman'. The French painter Claude Lorraine is said to have remarked that there were only two arts, painting and pastrycooking. Every culture has its own hierarchies and snobberies of the arts. In the classical world, oratory and rhetoric were rather high up on the list. In Europe today only painting and sculpture are given the elevated stature of 'fine arts'. The distinction between the supposedly higher and lower arts is largely a matter of function. Painting and sculpture can be regarded as the most unnecessary of the arts. They are luxuries, optional extras, function-free. This allows them to exist purely and simply as art and no other demands are made upon them.

So the expression 'artist-craftsman' has come to be used to signify those men and women who make objects in which the art element is uppermost with function of only secondary importance. Many an artist-craftsman uses his chosen medium, whether it be clay, weaving, or bookbinding, in much the same way that a painter uses paint, to express a personal idea. It was during the Renaissance that painters ceased to be regarded as plain tradesmen, following the dictates of the mainly religious functions of their art. It was then that personality came to the fore, and art began to be seen as a means of self-expression. In the same way there is a Renaissance now in some of the crafts, with a generation of intelligent craftsmen taking their particular crafts beyond the limitations of function and invading the exclusive and precious palaces of the 'fine arts'. Thus some works in clay are regarded not as pottery, but as 'ceramic sculpture'. And increasingly textiles are being made, not to be used, but as decorative wall-hangings to be enjoyed like paintings solely for their art. Although the artist-craftsmen are bringing a refreshing variety into the fine arts, the art establishment has still not quite absorbed these new recruits. Ceramic sculpture, for instance, is not usually exhibited in art galleries alongside other kinds of sculpture, nor has it been subjected to the intense analysis of the art critic. When it does come, however, this kind of recognition should have the effect of tightening up the artistic standards of the craftsmen as well as broadening the outlook of the art establishment itself.

Recognizing the growing influence of the crafts, the Minister responsible for the Arts set up the Crafts Advisory Committee in 1971. The committee was briefed to promote the interests of artist-craftsmen, and it has continued to perform this function with admirable vitality and style. It has funds to provide grants for practising craftsmen, helping them to rent workshop space, to train apprentices, to buy equipment, and in some cases to take sabbatical leave for travel and study. The Committee provides an information service that puts craftsmen in touch with prospective buyers; it organizes exhibitions of work and it publishes an excellent magazine, *Crafts,* which features some of the traditional as well as the more creative crafts.

Many of London's artist-craftsmen have enjoyed the support of the Crafts Advisory Committee, and have thus been cushioned to some extent against the pressures of the commercial world. The more traditional craftsmen, however, have not been so fortunate. Blacksmiths and bell-founders, coppersmiths and boat-builders—these are not classed as creative craftsmen and so they fall outside the scope of the Crafts Advisory Committee. Most of them must fend for themselves. Their businesses must be supported solely by the sale of their work. They cannot hope for grants to tide them over lean periods; no respite for experimentation and research. They must promote their own work and find their own clients, as well as carrying the responsibility of training the next generation in the trade.

There is one official body, based in London, that is intended to serve the interests of traditional craftsmen—but ironically its services are not available to Londoners. Called the Council for Small Industries in Rural Areas (CoSIRA) this organization runs training courses for several of the trades, and advises craftsmen on the management of their businesses. But CoSIRA was set up specifically to help rural craftsmen, and it can only offer help to a London firm or individual who is proposing to leave London and move out into the country. Some tradesmen, such as farriers, goldsmiths and silversmiths, may receive support from their City Livery companies. And in some areas of London, such as Clerkenwell and Soho, associations have been set up to promote the interests of local craftsmen. But the majority of London's traditional craftsmen can expect no help or advice from any benevolent organization.

These are tough times for small businesses. For a craftsman working on his own or at the head of a small firm, the mundane problems of running a business can seriously disrupt his work. The tax system is so complex that a sizeable proportion of his time must be spent on paperwork; everything he buys, everything he sells, must be recorded for the Value Added Tax inspector. Bureaucracy inhibits enterprise; many craftsmen are put off exporting their work by the amount of form-filling and restrictions that are involved.

Finding and holding onto workshop space is the biggest problem that craftsmen have to face in London today. The massive rent and rates rises in recent years have made it impossible for many firms to remain in premises that they have occupied for generations. In the property boom of the late 1960s and early 1970s some landlords were unscrupulous in their methods of clearing buildings of unprofitable small businesses so that the premises could be converted for luxury office use. There have been cases of craftsmen being forced out of their workshops by eviction orders that had no validity in law. In one case a tailor, whose tenancy was protected, was harassed by the landlord's agents, who even made holes in the roof to make life uncomfortable for him: finally he gave up his resistance and left London for good.

When one craftsman goes out of business others often suffer, since so many of the trades are mutually dependent. The architectural sculptor, for instance, depends upon the edge-tool maker who forges his stone chisels. For centuries craftsmen of related trades have tended to congregate in particular districts of London: watchmakers and jewellers, for instance, in Clerkenwell, tailors in Soho and woodworkers in Shoreditch. This arrangement favours the specialist so that different workshops can concentrate on different branches of the trade. A piece of furniture will be made by one firm in Shoreditch, veneered by another, and polished by a third. But as soon as one firm goes out of business or moves away, the circle is broken; now each firm must carry out more functions itself. Thus the modern craftsman is forced to become a Jack-of-all-trades, not through choice, but because he cannot call upon the services of his fellow-craftsmen.

The continuity of the crafts depends upon a reliable system of training the next generation of craftsmen. This century has seen social and educational changes that have radically altered the status of the craftsman and recruitment of apprentices into the trades. Right up to the Second World War the system of indentured apprenticeship prevailed. Craftsmen were regarded as the élite of working society and at times of low employment a craftsman could be sure of a reliable job. So a craft training was at a premium and parents who wanted their sons to get on in the world were happy to pay for their indentures. A master craftsman would receive a respectable sum for taking on an apprentice; and during the term of the apprenticeship, usually seven years, the craftsman would pay the apprentice only a low wage, rising in proportion to his usefulness. Today the last of the craftsmen who served this traditional apprenticeship are reaching retirement age. They have lived to see their status in society eroded; some of them are now among the lowest earners in the community. Today the craftsman is not paid to take on an apprentice; on the contrary he must pay a trainee a statutory minimum wage from the day he joins the workshop. It is not surprising that many of the older craftsmen are bitter about the change in the system that has made them pay out at both ends of their careers.

The older craftsmen are also critical of the calibre of the school-leavers who are entering the workshops today. Their disapproval is partly the reaction of a rigidly disciplined older generation to a relaxed and liberated youth. But there is another basis for it too: the huge improvements in education, and equal opportunities for all, have meant that a very high proportion of intelligent and talented individuals go on from school to higher education in universities and colleges. Only the less able school-leavers tend to be directed towards the trades. Before higher education became so widely available there was a broader range of ability in school-leavers who went straight into work; and competition among them was intense so that only the best were taken on as apprentices to master craftsmen.

There are opportunities for learning certain crafts within the higher education system. Ceramics, textiles, bookbinding, glassmaking and furniture design—these are well taught at art schools. Here the emphasis is on design and creative self-expression rather than practical techniques. Within the art schools there are technicians who carry out the more complex procedures for the students. Consequently, out of the 22,000-odd students attending full-time art courses at any one time, only a small proportion come out at the age of 21 or so with a really practical ability in their chosen specialities. So employers are sometimes justified in complaining that they find art school graduates impractical, opinionated and unwilling to do their share of the mundane jobs.

Practical courses in certain trades such as tailoring, clockmaking, shoemaking and furniture manufacture are available at several technical colleges in the London area. But for a large number of the trades, such as gunmaking, coppersmithing or taxidermy, there are no training schemes, no systems of apprenticeship and no central organizations to process inquiries and applications. The only way that a young person can learn these trades is to be born into a craftsman's family, to pick up the trade on a hobby basis, or to persuade a practising craftsman to take him on. This last course rarely succeeds because not many craftsmen are willing to sacrifice time and output to teach their trade.

What is needed is a subsidized system of apprenticeship that would serve all the trades. Quite simply, master craftsmen in all fields should be paid to take on apprentices. The payment should be sufficient to compensate for their loss of earnings, with a little bit extra as an incentive. The apprentices themselves should receive grants on a par with those given to students on academic courses. A practical workshop training in the crafts ought to command the same prestige as a college education. A public subsidy towards the crafts trades would be a recognition of the contribution that craftsmen make, not only to the quality of our lives, but also to the nation's economy. As long as 'London best' continues to signify the highest standards of craftsmanship, foreign visitors will continue to come and buy in London. And as long as there is a market for well-made goods there will be Londoners who find fulfilment making them.

The Craft Guilds in London

The growth of the City of London in wealth and power is closely tied up with the rise of the guilds of tradesmen who carried out their trade within the City's walls. These guilds, which have survived to this day in the form of the City Livery Companies, wielded immense power in their day. They were exclusive societies which served as rigid guardians over the standards of their trade. They dealt out privileges to those who conformed, but their disapproval was to spell doom for many a craftsman's career.

The trade guilds of London can be traced right back to the 'frith-gilds' of Saxon times. The frith-gilds were like mutual protection societies, formed from family groups and having power to police the community and to punish offenders. These groups grew into local religious fraternities. Having no meeting houses, they gathered together in the local church or monastery. Hence they came to adopt the local parish saint as patron.

The connection with the trades was accidental at first and developed only gradually. The members of a particular trade tended to congregate within a small area of London and inevitably the local guilds came to be made up predominantly of members of a single trade. The tailors were based around Birchin Lane, the basket-makers in Pudding Lane, drapers in Candlewick and salters in Bread Street. The members of each guild carried on business with each other and supported each other against outside competition. So the guilds, which had started out with a religious complexion, came to represent the interests of the separate trades or 'misteries' as they were called (mistery—from the French, *métier*). The merchant guilds, like the Fishmongers, Grocers and Merchant Taylors, represented the retail tradesmen, and the craft guilds, like the Goldsmiths, Cordwainers, Armourers and Saddlers stood for the craftsmen. The religious origin of the City guilds was never completely lost, and to this day the City companies have kept the name of their patron saint in the official title; the Goldsmiths' Company for instance are known as 'Goldsmiths of St Dunstan' and the Saddlers as 'Saddlers of St Martin'.

The early days of the trade guilds were fraught with disputes which were usually taken to the Lord Mayor for arbitration. For instance, in the City archives of 1309 it is reported that 'much damage was happening daily to the great Lords and people of the land by reason of deceits employed in making saddles'. The saddlers of London were brought before the Lord Mayor, but they passed the buck on to the joiners who were responsible for making the wooden framework (the bow) on which the saddles were built. It transpired that 'naughty apprentices who had run away from their masters, with other deceitful men did resort to the woods which were close to the City and did there patch up saddle bows in the roughest and most deceitful manner possible'. The parts were made with green unseasoned wood and under cover of night they would be smuggled into the City and passed on to dishonest saddlers who would paint them or cover them up with cloth and offer them for sale. As the wood dried, it shrank; the saddle collapsed and the innocent rider, it was reported, was thrown off.

As a result of all this the Lord Mayor decided that the members of the two 'misteries' should have the power to search and stamp all goods with their mark. Saddle painters were not allowed to paint any saddle bow made outside the City until it had been approved by jurors appointed by the Mistery of Joiners. No joiners were allowed to work in the woods after this, and any faulty goods were taken to the Guildhall where they were officially condemned, and from there to Westchepe where they were publicly burned.

The powers of the trade guilds to search for and condemn faulty goods were made law when the guilds were set up as City Livery Companies from the reign of Edward I onwards. The membership of each Company was originally restricted to members of the trade and they were allowed to wear the uniform or 'livery' of the Company. By 1423 there were over a hundred separate Companies. They were exclusive societies with broad powers of control over their trades. They ran closed shops and did not allow outsiders to carry on trade in London. If a liveryman was guilty of bad work he was stripped of his livery and banned from working in the City. This may be the origin of the expression 'sent to Coventry', because Coventry was the city closest to London where an outlawed tradesman could freely set up business again.

The duty of the City Companies to stamp goods with their mark of approval survives today with the 'hallmark' which, by law, has to be stamped upon all pieces of gold, silver and platinum offered for sale in Britain. The word 'hallmark' originally meant the mark applied at Goldsmiths' Hall, as the Goldsmiths' Company had the exclusive responsibility of assaying the nation's precious metal. Now there are assay offices in several cities, controlled by a central assay board, but the London assay office is still at Goldsmiths' Hall. The Company employs over one hundred people in its assay department and in any one year they expect to hallmark over seven million items. The hallmark is not a judgement of the quality of craftsmanship: it is a certificate of the purity of the metal.

Another area in which the City Companies had a strict influence was in the training of apprentices. Nobody could set up as a craftsman unless he had served a full apprenticeship, as a statute from Elizabethan times very elaborately states:

'It shall not be laufull to any person or persons other than suche as nowe do laufully use or exercise any Arte, Misterye or Manuell Occupacon to sette uppe, occupie, use or exercise anye Crafte Misterye or Occupacon nowe used or occupied within the realms of Englande or Wales Excepte he shall have been brought uppe therein seaven yeares at the least as Apprentice in maner and forme abovesaid.'

Before a lad could become an apprentice he had to be brought before the Wardens of his Company who examined him to see 'wether hee bee a freeborn subject of the King of England or not' and 'wether hee bee cleane and whole lymed [limbed].'

The rules and conditions of apprenticeship were strictly laid down. A boy's father had to pay a sizeable fee to a master craftsman to take on his son, and a proportion of the boy's earnings went automatically to the master. The boy was bound by a solemn written agreement, or indenture, to serve his master for a period of seven years. The craftsman undertook to feed and clothe the apprentice, and usually to provide a home for him under his own roof. The master became the physical and moral guardian of his apprentice. A nineteenth-century instruction from the Farriers' Company to all apprentices makes it clear where their loyalties should lie:

'You shall constantly and devoutly on your knees every day serve God and make conscience on the due hearing of His word preached and endeavour the right practice thereof in your life and conversation . . . When you have leisure, go to Church . . . Avoid all evil company; always make speedy return when you shall have been sent on your master's errands; avoid idleness and always be employed either in God's service, or in your master's business.'

At the end of his apprenticeship the young craftsman had to submit a proof of his proficiency, a 'masterpiece', to his Company. If this was judged to be of high enough quality then the craftsman was made a fully qualified 'journeyman', and admitted to the Freedom of his Company. Again, the Goldsmiths' Company has kept up this tradition. To this day, master goldsmiths and silversmiths who are Freemen of the Company send their apprentices to the Hall to apply for their own Freedom when their training is complete. To qualify as a master craftsman, the apprentice has to show his masterpiece to the Company. Once he has been elected to the Freedom of the Company the craftsman can apply for the Freedom of the City of London.

The strict rules of apprenticeship made the craftsmen an exclusive group. Any exclusive circle of people tends to conjure up rituals which serve to emphasize their exclusiveness, and so it was with the craftsmen. The entry of a qualified young apprentice into the trade was an excuse for some extraordinary junketings. To this day in some workshops of the silver trade, the newly qualified craftsman is still expected to stand on his head at his bench, to the accompaniment of the greatest cacophony that his workmates can muster by beating their metal tools together. In the coopering trade within living memory the admission ritual seemed brutally designed as a final test of a young man's stamina before he was allowed to come of age as a craftsman. The initiation ceremony, known as the 'trusso', is described by Bob Gilding in his book *The Journeyman Coopers of East London*.

On the day of the 'trusso' the young man begins to make a cask, but before it is finished his colleagues lift him up and throw him into it. They drive the metal hoops home to hold it together and then proceed to roll the cask, with the unfortunate lad inside, the whole length of the yard. He is spun several times and rolled back and up-ended. A mixture of sawdust and wood ash is poured over the boy. Now his master walks up to the cask, with a pint of beer in each hand, and offers him a drink. The boy always accepts, whereupon one pint is poured over his head. He is allowed to stand up and drink the other. He is then handed his cards and formally dismissed from his job. Ritual demands that he should then apply for a new job as a journeyman cooper, and in this way he is accepted into the fold.

Bob Gilding has another description which provides a rich insight into the occasional stuffy and cruel pride of the tradesmen, which continued well into the twentieth century. Gilding was fourteen years old, an apprentice in his first week at work. He had been told to ask the coopers in the workshop how many hoops they required for the day's work. The first time he asked a question there was no reply:

'Raising my voice I asked the same question again. Again there was no reply, but this time the largest of the coopers, a really huge man, turned on me. He placed his apron carefully over the nearest barrel, picked me up by the hair of my head, carried me across the shop and shut the door in my face. All this was done in grave silence . . . The second morning was a replica of the first, as was the third and fourth. By the fifth day I was becoming so desperate, partly from pain but mainly because nobody would explain the purpose of the ritual, that I determined to discover the reason or leave the cooperage. Plucking up my courage I entered the shop, asked my usual question and then dodged behind a barrel, demanding to know why I was being so harshly treated. Very calmly the large cooper informed me that anyone entering a cooper's shop had to say "Good morning, gentlemen all," just as anyone leaving at night had to say "Good night, gentlemen all." Having said that he made a grab at me, lifted me clean over the barrel and once again carried me across the shop by my hair . . .'

This kind of hollow ritual represents the decay of a tradition of exclusiveness which had begun in the noble cause of ensuring high standards. From the Middle Ages to the industrial revolution, the influence of some of the City Companies had declined. This was largely due to the disappearance of the crafts that they represented. Companies like the Armourers and Braziers, the Gold and Silver Wyre Drawers, the Pattenmakers (pattens were wooden shoe covers, like galoshes, worn to protect the shoes from mud), the Bowyers and Fletchers, found themselves with scarcely any craftsmen left. Other Companies weakened their influence by allowing people unconnected with their trade to join; in most Companies, liverymen were allowed to elect their sons even if they did not follow the same profession. Paradoxically the Companies' influence reached its lowest level in the nineteenth century when their accumulated wealth was at its highest.

With no responsibilities remaining, some of the Companies had little to do but squander their wealth. Even in an era when all kinds of excesses were tolerated, the expenditure of the City Companies on their own comforts met with hostile criticism. They were charged with spending their income on gourmandising, and they were said to have ceased to perform any useful function in the modern state. It was proposed that their charters be revoked and their funds appropriated for more useful purposes. These rumblings continued for several years before, in 1880, a Royal Commission was set up, with Lord Derby as chairman, to look into the expenditure by the Companies on their hospitality.

Lord Derby's report was inconclusive, but even before his commission sat, the Companies had acted upon the criticisms that had been levelled against them. In 1878 the City Corporation and the City Livery Companies gave funds for a highly important new organization to provide education in the craft trades—the City and Guilds Institute. The Institute was the brainchild of the great biologist T. H. Huxley who saw the need for craft workers to be educated in the principles of technology and design. The City and Guilds College of Engineering was set up at South Kensington and still survives as part of Imperial College, now under the control of the University of London. But the City and Guilds is best known by its examinations, which set the standards of education in technical colleges. City and Guilds qualifications are recognized by employers the world over. No fewer than two hundred subjects are covered by the examinations, with up to three levels of qualifications in each. The subjects range from sewing to clockmaking, from farriery to baking. The Institute is still funded in part by grants from the Corporation of the City of London and from the City Livery Companies, but its income from examination fees makes it almost independent.

The City and Guilds Art School in Kennington is quite separate from the City and Guilds Institute, although it too was founded by the City Corporation and Companies and continues to be supported by them. As well as providing courses in painting and sculpture, the City and Guilds is one of the few schools where students can learn restoration, gilding and lettering.

At the present time the independence of the City Corporation is being challenged by critics who argue that the City should come under the jurisdiction of the Greater London Council, just like any other London borough. In the present debate the City institutions, which include the Livery Companies, are once again coming under close scrutiny. It is clear that while certain companies, such as the Goldsmiths', continue to fulfil their responsibilities to their trades, others have grown away from their original purposes. It remains to be seen whether the charitable and ceremonial activities of these Companies are sufficient justification for their continued survival into the late twentieth century.

PART II

Metalworkers

London has little of the large-scale metal industry that is to be found in the Midlands and the North. Light engineering and precision metalwork are characteristic. Mr Welford, the last man in London to forge the links of chains by hand, gave up the work in 1973, but still one finds small firms of coppersmiths, farriers, blacksmiths, many with forges hidden somewhat incongruously between the houses of quiet residential streets . . .

Blacksmith

'We do a bit of anything as long as it's ironwork': thus Irving Benbow, a third-generation London blacksmith, accounts for his firm's survival in the same premises for over a hundred years. The business is very much a family concern. As well as his own son, three of Mr Benbow's cousins work with him at his smithy off the Walworth Road, and only the apprentice is not one of the family. Since Mr Benbow's grandfather opened the shop in 1874, the blacksmith's trade has seen so many changes that it has been only the most resilient and adaptable smiths who have stayed in business.

A century ago, the urban blacksmith was kept busy with decorative ironwork such as gates, railings and window grilles, fittings for shop signs, park seats and fireplaces, as well as making tools for craftsmen of other trades. The blacksmith was usually the local farrier as well, and spent a lot of his time shoeing horses. There was enough work in every district to sustain at least one blacksmith and his mate. Today the same range of work exists but there is hardly enough of it in the whole of London to keep a single blacksmith in business. The modern blacksmith has to find new outlets for his work, and over the years the Benbow family has been very successful at this.

Until about ten years ago the backbone of their trade was fitting metal bands, called tyres, on the wooden wheels of costermongers' market barrows. Iron strips would be bent and the ends hammered together while hot to make a tyre slightly smaller in diameter than the wheel that it was to fit. The tyre was heated in a furnace to expand it, and dropped over the wheel; the wheel was lowered into water, which quenched the heat of the metal, contracting it onto the wheel, and hardening it at the same time.

The work never really tailed off, but shrewdly the Benbows saw that in the long run it was doomed, as the craftsmen who made the wooden wheels were disappearing. Using the same techniques that they had used for tyres, they began to make metal rings which are needed for the framework of ventilation and air-conditioning systems. Still they used tools and techniques that would be familiar to any smith over the last three thousand years—a coal-burning forge ventilated by hand-operated bellows and a hammer and anvil to shape and to weld hot metal. The next stage in the adaptation process was the introduction of new techniques. The hand bellows went, and were replaced by an electric system: 'The old governor was convinced that the new blower was useless; he swore by the old hand bellows because he said he could control the heat better with them.' Even so, the forge itself was soon to become dispensable. A machine was bought that could bend the cold metal into shape. This saves a huge amount of time and brute strength, but does not altogether remove the element of skill, as the rings still have to be judged by eye and hammered straight by hand. For welding, the intense heat of an oxyacetylene flame is used. The surfaces to be welded are simply heated with the oxyacetylene torch and pressed together.

The new technology of the blacksmith's trade has not only increased the Benbows' productivity, it also leaves them with some energy and spare time for a little life outside the trade. When they were making metal tyres the working day used to begin at 4.30 a.m. and often did not finish till 10 at night. 'When Irving was getting married he was working on the Friday night till ten o'clock. He was married on the Saturday, had Sunday off, and was back at work first thing on Monday morning.' Nowadays Irving Benbow and his son drive up every morning from their home at Erith in Kent, getting to work at 6.30, an hour before their colleagues. But this is only because they like to take Friday afternoon off to play a round of golf.

Farrier

The farrier's job is shoeing horses. There are still a surprising number of working horses in the streets of London today—police horses, cavalry horses, heavy carthorses that pull the brewers' drays, the nags of rag-and-bone men or 'totters' not to mention the horses that are ridden for pleasure in Hyde Park, Richmond Park and on Wimbledon Common. Horses used regularly in the streets need to be re-shod once a month and horses that do very heavy work, like drawing brewers' drays, need new shoes every ten days or so. On the face of it then, there is plenty of work for a farrier in London. The army and the police employ their own farriers, and breweries like Young's and Whitbread's more or less monopolize the work of one or two others. But freelance independent farriers with their local forges have become very scarce.

The 1851 census showed that there were over 1,800 farriers in London. Street transport at the time was all horse-drawn and there were enough horses in every district to sustain a full-time local farrier. In the latest Telephone Directory only three farriers are listed within the Greater London telephone district. This figure is deceptively low because the number of farriers working in London is swollen by a number who travel in regularly from country districts.

The farrier today cannot hope to sustain his business on local trade. He has to service a wide area, and more often than not the farrier travels to the horse, and not the other way about. The modern farrier's forge and his toolkit are compact enough to be stowed in the back of a van.

One of the few surviving local forges is run by Bill Geddes in Battersea. Bill

Geddes' father started up as a farrier in Battersea in 1906, and the family moved to the present forge in Chivalry Road in 1942 after the original forge site was bombed in the blitz. For two days a week Bill Geddes is out on the road, shoeing under contract at riding stables, but the rest of the time he is at Chivalry Road, and depends on local trade. Many of the South London totters bring their horses to him. He makes no appointments and has no idea who is coming from one day to the next. But all his customers are regulars, and he knows roughly when to expect them. So if he has a quiet period he uses the time to make up shoes in advance.

'On Monday I had only one. So I spent the day making shoes. Tuesday I was going all day and I didn't even have time to stop and make a cup of tea. I had nine altogether that day.'

One of the farrier's skills is to make the horse relax and co-operate with him. He starts work at the front legs and persuades the horse to lift one leg by gently tugging at the fringe of hair around the hoof. Now the farrier stoops down into his working position, with his back against the horse's shoulder, the horse's leg between his knees and its foot resting on the lap of his leather apron. In this position he can rest his weight against the horse's upper leg. Both horse and man are comfortable and the horse cannot lift its leg up further to kick him.

He clears the hood of mud and dirt and prises off the old shoe with his pincers. Beneath the shoe the horse's hoof has grown like a vast toe-nail and the next job is to pare this down with a sharp blade. He deals with each hoof in turn.

Next, he takes a set of new shoes, made earlier for this particular horse, and stacks them neatly in the fire of the forge, raking hot coals around them. When the shoes are red-hot he takes one out of the fire on a pair of tongs, casually lights his cigarette on the glowing metal, hammers the shoe on the anvil, and jabs a sharp spike or 'punch' into the base of it. Now, gripping the punch with the shoe attached, he takes one of the horse's feet in his lap and presses the red-hot shoe against the hoof. Acrid yellow smoke from the burning hoof rises into the farrier's face and he blows a channel through it to see what is happening. The horse feels no pain as the horny material of the hoof has no nerves. The reason for burning the shoe onto the hoof is to ensure that the surface of the hoof is absolutely flat and also to check that the shoe is a proper fit. While the shoe is still hot he carries out any necessary changes at the anvil before plunging the shoe into a tank of water to cool. Each shoe is marked so that he knows which foot it belongs to. He nails the shoes on to the hooves with heavily tapered farrier's nails, using a hammer with small head and a slender, slightly whippy handle.

Finally the farrier deals with the upper surfaces of the hooves. Resting one of the horse's feet on a metal tripod, he files off the protruding points of the nails and the discoloured surface of the hoof, and paints on a dark lubricating lotion compounded of linseed oil, paraffin and various other ingredients. His chiropody complete, the horse is ready to clatter out of the workshop on a smart new set of shoes.

For Bill Geddes' regular customers the visit to the forge means much more than a monthly pedicure for their horses. It is a chance for them to catch up on the news and gossip of the horse trade. Throughout the hour or so that it takes to shoe a horse Bill Geddes keeps up a constant conversation with the owner, although he hardly ever looks up from his work.

Edge-tool Maker

Some of the honours that have gone to our distinguished sculptors and stonecarvers ought to be reserved for the man who made their tools. Harold Pound has been making carvers' edge-tools for over sixty years and is as distinguished in his own trade as many a sculptor of greater fame and glory. He has been the last edge-tool maker in London for many years. Now over eighty, he does a full day's work at his anvil with energy that would be remarkable in a man half his age.

Henry Moore, Epstein, Barbara Hepworth, all have used Harold Pound's tools, and so have the unknown carvers and letterers who have decorated London's buildings and monuments. The lettering on the Cenotaph was done with Harold Pound's tools. The stonemasons and carvers at St Paul's use them. His work is known outside England too and he tells with some delight how, on a trip to Oberammergau, he found that the carvers there were using tools that he had made.

If he had not become a toolmaker, Harold Pound would have been a musician. His sense of rhythm shows up in his work, and over the years his working routine has developed into a kind of regular rhythmical dance. His whole body moves in time to the motion of the handle of the forge bellows, which he winds with his left hand while prodding at the fire with his right. When he hammers a tool into shape on his anvil, he builds up a rhythm that he cannot stop. When he pauses to inspect his work, he does not stop hammering but continues beating out the rhythm on the anvil until directing the hammer back to the tool itself.

The raw material for an edge-tool is a bar of cast steel about half an inch in diameter. Mr Pound cuts the bar into nine-inch lengths with a home-made contraption in which a hacksaw is worked by a small electric motor. He heats the tip of the bar to red-heat in his forge. The hot steel is shaped into a flat, pointed, or V-shaped tool with blows of the hammer on the edge-tool maker's anvil. He shapes the hot tip of the steel against the anvil by carefully controlled blows of the hammer. He makes stonecarvers' chisels of assorted widths, flattening the metal with the hammer and finishing off the sharp edges with a file. Some tools he tapers down to a point; others, called claw tools, are like flat chisels with nicks filed at intervals so that the tips look like outstretched hands. He judges the width of his chisel edges by eye and rarely has to take a measurement.

The test of a good tool-maker is whether his tools are hard enough to remain sharp for a long time, but not so brittle that they snap when working. His skill lies in catching the metal at precisely the correct temperature for working, and cooling it in just the right way to harden it. Mr Pound is masterly at judging the state of the metal from its colour. Each length of steel has different qualities; even pieces cut from the same bar may be different. If the metal is too hot from the forge he dips the reverse end in water to cool it down a bit. He tempers the tip of a tool with water which he may just touch onto a particular spot with a wet cloth. Everything has to be done at speed while the metal is in the correct state for working.

Mr Pound's workshop is in a hidden corner of London which the twentieth century seems to have passed by, unregarded. Certainly it is a corner where decimalization and metrication seem unlikely to reach. It is not just the appearance of the place and the man, both of which could have been lifted from a nineteenth-century engraving. Harold Pound's pride in his work and his old-world courtesies and manners are noticeable because they are so rare in younger people. The decline in standards that he sees around him makes him critical. But he criticizes cheerfully and with the authority of a man whose own standards have been maintained at the highest level for the sixty years of his working life. He often criticizes the British workman, but he still gives a tip to the man who delivers his coal and who earns almost twice as much as he does himself.

Wire-worker

Mr Hunter's ancestors have been wire-workers since 1770 and he still works in the same premises in Hackney where his grandfather and father worked before him. Garden sieves, letter-cages, rat-traps and flower baskets are Mr Hunter's line of business and he weaves the wire mesh for them by hand with a hand-made loom.

To prepare a length of wire for weaving it has first to be fed into a hand-operated crimping machine, which creates waves in the wire. The loom (known as a 'broom' in the trade) is a surprisingly simple device, made of wire with a wooden handle. Five-foot lengths of waved wire are threaded into loops on the loom. Half the wires point upwards, half point down. By turning the loom on its side the arrangement is reversed. So the craftsman weaves by threading a short length of wire between the two sets of longer wires, turning the loom, weaving another wire, and so on.

Mr Hunter works at a speed that comes from a lifetime's experience.

'My father lived next door to this shop. I was born there and I'm fifty-five now, so you could say I've been here all my life. I've been learning it since I was ten years old. When I got home from school I used to go into the workshop. I left school when I was fourteen and I've been here ever since. The hours were longer in them days. We used to work from eight in the morning till seven at night.

Skilled wire-workers are hard to find these days. The boys today aren't interested. I used to employ three boys; some of them stopped here three or four years, but I couldn't keep them any longer. Also the factory inspector said that things had to be done to the premises if I was to employ people; they were too dilapidated.

I'd say that 95 per cent of my work now is letter-cages. I do eight different sizes, from this small household one here, right up to the larger ones for factories. I have a run of flower baskets in the spring and then they're over. Sieves are going off: they take longer to make and there's not the call for them now. The price of the wood and the galvanized metal has gone up; and the wire that I used for sieves is a fantastic price. So this is the last lot of that wire I'll get in. When that's finished, it'll be the end of the sieve side. Today you have to turn out what sells best.'

There are several other craftsmen in London working with wire. They tend to specialize in one particular line, such as lampshade frames, wire baskets and the like.

Coppersmith

In Whitfield Street, just south of the Euston Road, there is a shopfront that reads 'Boscacci Moresi; coppersmiths and re-tinners'. Behind the façade the floor is sunk well below ground level and one steps down into a choking subterranean air, dense with the fumes of chemicals rising from tanks against the walls, and smoke from the open forge. The workshop is open to the roof, which is pierced by a skylight so blackened with dust that it has long ceased to allow light through. But one pane is broken and through this a shaft of sunlight creates a white channel through the escaping smoke. A steel girder crossing the room supports a huge fan which has seized up under its burden of soot. Below, and covering almost all the space on the floor, is a haphazard accumulation of pots of all shapes and sizes; and on shelves against the wall, fish fryers, sieves, potato-mashers and the like, all abandoned.

There have been wire-workers in the Hunter family since 1770. The present Mr Hunter has the same Hackney workshop where his father and grandfather made garden sieves, rat-traps and letter-cages before him.

Bill Geddes, the Battersea farrier. His forge is one of the few where London's rag-and-bone men can come to have their nags attended to. Working horses need to be re-shod once a month. All Bill Geddes' customers are regulars and he has a new set of shoes ready for each one in advance. In a casual reflex action the farrier lights his cigarette from a red-hot horseshoe. He burns the shoe onto the horse's hoof to ensure that the shoe is a proper fit. The horse feels no pain, as the hoof is dead material, like a fingernail.

The edge-tool maker. Harold Pound has been making tools for stone-carvers and sculptors for over sixty years. His customers have included Jacob Epstein, Barbara Hepworth and Henry Moore as well as the architectural sculptors of St Paul's. For many years the last toolmaker in London, Mr Pound has no apprentices, and when he retires his forge at Vauxhall will be flattened for a playground.

The cooper. Shaving the outside of a barrel is an unconventional task for Tom Wood, the cooper at Young's Brewery in Wandsworth. Usually the cooper has to shave the inside of the barrel to remove any impurities that might taint the beer. But this particular barrel is destined for decorative use and so the shaving is purely cosmetic.

A marquetry maker and his display. Mr Fisher puts this sample board outside his Shoreditch shop on the rare occasions that he is short of work. He provides classical marquetry embellishments for many of the cabinet-makers in the area. Like many craftsmen he is motivated by the pleasure of producing fine work: 'I enjoy every job I do.'

The cabinet-maker, one of a team of craftsmen employed in Bill Marney's clock and barometer firm on the edge of Clerkenwell. This case for a grandmother clock is finished in flame mahogany veneer. The fluted pillars at the top were turned on a lathe by another craftsman in the same workshop. Hanging at the back are new-made barometer cases.

Covent Garden barrow makers. The firm of Ellen Keeley has stayed in Covent Garden, although the market, for which their barrows were made, has moved away. They hire out their barrows to market stallholders all over London, as well as supplying them as television props. Market barrows are always hired, not sold, and so barrow makers carve their names to identify their property. They have a unique style of lettering, flowery and free-flowing, which they carve at great speed. Here Terry O'Doherty, a great-grandson of the Irish lady who started the firm, demonstrates his technique. The sample carving above was made by one of the family of the previous generation.

The best cooks like to use pots and pans of copper with an inside lining of tin. The copper is sturdy and conducts the heat well, and the tin supplies a hard inner lining that prevents the food becoming adulterated with copper. These days copper pans are mass-produced in factories, but the old hand-made ones are much treasured by the chefs who use them. They will last for ages if they are properly looked after. Some of the pans used at Queen Victoria's coronation feast come to Boscacci Moresi for maintenance. And the firm looks after the pans of many of the top London restaurants, hotels and clubs.

There used to be eleven men working here but now there are only two, Mr Marchetti, son-in-law of one of the Moresi family, and his assistant. Mr Marchetti hammers out dented pans, replaces missing handles, and mends holes by patching with molten copper. But the bulk of his work is re-tinning. Before the metal will accept a new layer of tin it needs to be thoroughly cleaned of all traces of grease. The pan is soaked in a series of tanks of caustic soda at various heats and strengths. After this treatment the copper is sparkling as new, and ready for tinning. Mr Marchetti brushes a suspension of chalk around the outer rim of the pot, to prevent the tin from attaching itself there, and then sets the pot, bottom uppermost, on the fire. When the metal has reached the right heat he turns the pan with tongs, and, keeping the base on the fire, wipes a stick of metallic tin around the inside of the pan. The tin melts with the heat and forms a thin plating all over the interior of the pan. To cool the tin, and harden it, he brushes water over it, raising clouds of steam. Now the whole pot is washed again and dried in a barrel of sawdust. The coppersmith takes three hours or so over each pan.

Mr Marchetti has lived in England most of his life, but he speaks with a strong Italian accent. 'We can't get the young people to join this trade; it's dirty work and the fumes are bad, especially when it's damp weather. These trades are dying out because the young people will have nothing to do with them. They can get jobs in factories where they don't have to learn anything. Here you take years to learn the trade. We get so much work we have to turn it away. I'm sixty-six and I'll pack it up when the lease expires. We should have been out by last year, but we've hung on, and now we've been told we must be out by Christmas.'

As this book goes to press, the coppersmith's lease has expired, Mr Marchetti's family business is finished and the shop derelict. At last the grimy skylight is open to the sky. The workshop where pans were sealed with tin is itself sealed with an impenetrable façade of corrugated iron.

PART III

Precious metals

The working properties of silver and gold as well as their rarity has made these metals the chosen vehicles for fine craftsmanship in most great civilizations. Both are highly malleable—easy to hammer out. Gold can be spread out by hammering until it is only a few atoms thick. Flat sheets of silver can be hammered into depressions in wood or against rounded tools to make hollow shapes. Both metals can be drawn out to make wire; they can be bent, cut, engraved, inlaid with other materials. They can be melted and the molten metal poured into prepared moulds i.e., cast, to make any required shape. Separate pieces of gold and silver can be assembled by soldering. Repeated shapes, such as medals, can be made by stamping out sheet metal with a die. The versatility of these materials gives the craftsman almost unlimited scope.

Gold-beater

The point of beating gold is to hammer out the metal into extremely fine leaves. Gold is the most malleable of metals; it can be beaten into a layer only 1/250,000 of an inch thick. As gold leaf it is used by carvers, bookbinders, scribes and illuminators to provide an infinitesimally thin skin of pure gold to cover their work.

It was not very long ago that the gold-beater had to stand all day at a bench lifting a 12 lb. hammer above his head and bringing it down on a package containing small squares of gold. It is a relief for all concerned that such endurance is no longer required of the gold-beater, as there are machines to do some of the heavy work for him. All the same, the ancient skills of gold-beating have not been lost: they survive still in one firm in England, George Whiley of Ruislip.

To design a machine that does the work of a craftsman, Whiley's engineers strapped lights to the hammer, wrist and arm of a gold-beater and photographed him in action. The machine that resulted has such a complex range of movements—the position and angle of the hammer is varied with every blow—that it provides clear proof of the gold-beater's traditional skills. These skills are still maintained by a small group of craftsmen who do the final beating of each batch of gold leaf by hand.

At Whiley's a bar of solid gold is put through a machine which rolls it into a long ribbon. The ribbon is cut into two-inch squares and the squares are interleaved with larger squares of vellum. Two hundred squares each of gold and vellum are made into a package or 'cutch' which is ready for the first beating. The hammer is mechanised, but the cutch is moved by hand between each blow so that a different area of the gold is beaten with every blow. After twenty minutes the gold squares have been spread out until they reach the edges of the vellum. Each square is now divided into four and 800 of these smaller squares are interleaved with very fine paper and made into a cutch for the second beating. The process is repeated, and each square of gold is subjected to four beatings altogether. The final beating is finished off by hand.

The gold-beater strikes with a characteristic action of the wrist, giving a glancing blow which is designed to spread out the gold under the hammer. He settles into a rhythm and makes the hammer do much of the work itself, bouncing back under its own momentum. He holds the package of gold with the fingers of his left hand and spins it after each blow, so that a different area of gold is beaten every time, and the gold is hammered out evenly. The skill in gold-beating lies in using a very heavy tool to do a very delicate job. The delicate gold leaf can be split by one badly placed blow, and the gold-beater has to adjust his action as the temperature of the gold builds up under the hammering.

The final hammering complete, the gold is taken out of the packages leaf by leaf by a woman skilled in the craft. Each leaf is so fine and light that the slightest puff of air can crumple it. By rubbing her boxwood pincers against her hair, the craftswoman creates a slight electrostatic charge which is enough to lift a single leaf of gold. With a well-aimed puff of breath she settles the leaf onto a leather pad. Now she cuts the leaf into a perfect square, using a 'wagon', a little boxwood tool with two parallel blades of split cane which serve as cutting edges. Another deft movement with the pincers, a puff of breath, and the finished leaf of gold is laid on a sheet of tissue paper. Packed into books of twenty-five, the leaves of gold are ready for sale.

Silversmith

Great credit for the untarnished health of this trade is due to the Goldsmiths' Company which controls the standards of the craft as much as it did in the Middle Ages. The Company is generous with prizes, scholarships and commissions. It organizes apprenticeship schemes and gives financial help to master craftsmen and apprentices who need it. Before admission as a master craftsman, the apprentice silversmith submits a 'masterpiece' to the Company for inspection. On qualifying, he receives his freedom of the Company, and outstanding silversmiths are elected to the full membership or 'Livery' of the Company.

In London now there are several thousand craftsmen making a living from silver work, and hundreds more practising the craft part-time as a hobby. Fortunately there are still customers for the more ambitious pieces of silver, including jewellery, and the top London silversmiths receive many commissions for presentation salvers, bowls, sporting trophies for major events, ecclesiastical and table silver and so on. True, the patronage of the English Establishment may have somewhat declined, but foreign patrons, largely from the Middle East, have stepped in to make up for it, so that a large proportion of the London silversmiths' production is exported.

One silversmith who has had a lion's share of official commissions as well as foreign patronage is Stuart Devlin. An Australian-born craftsman, he first came to England to study at the Royal College of Art and, after a series of travel scholarships, came to settle in London. His list of commissions ranges from designs for the Australian coinage to cutlery for the President of France; from the Grand National Trophy to the altar cross for Canterbury Cathedral. His workshops are in Clerkenwell, traditionally a centre of the silversmith's trade, and he has built around him a nucleus of craftsmen, now numbering fifty-five.

Devlin is something of a Renaissance figure. Eclectic, a man of the world, a shrewd businessman, an organiser as well as a craftsman, his success has meant that he makes progressively fewer of his pieces himself, but entrusts more and more of the making to his team of specialist craftsmen. Every piece that leaves the workshop is designed by Devlin. His output is prodigious, and extraordinarily versatile. One craftsman is employed full-time carrying out his jewellery designs; another takes charge of the hollow-ware—goblets, bowls and the like; another specializes in small work, which means here the luxuriantly embellished golden eggs that are a Devlin speciality. There is a full-time spoonmaker and a craftsman making models for coins and medals. As if all these activities were not enough, Stuart Devlin has recently opened a furniture workshop. His furniture designs, like those of his silver, are highly decorative. "I wanted to introduce a new idiom into furniture design—there's no rich furniture being made any more. I want it to be rich, but contemporary."

For Stuart Devlin, speed of production is an important element of success:

'Our contribution has been to develop techniques that enable us to do things more quickly. Most people think that our success has been aesthetic. Really it is entirely technical; techniques have created their own aesthetic.

We have a lot of commissions for coins and medals. The monopoly used to be with the French craftsmen who took about five weeks to make a plaster model. But my lad does five in a week. It's because we don't put "art" above craftsmanship. We don't call ourselves 'artists' with a capital A.

The most expensive factor used to be the metal; but now the biggest expense is the craftsman's time. Anyone can be highly skilled if they have time. Now the need is to produce highly skilled work within very tight time limits. We have an unusual number of machine tools—they give a silversmith a flexibility that he used not to have. He can work more quickly.

We'd like to get our apprentices when they're twelve—but we're not allowed to, so we get them at sixteen when they leave school. We have to get them early so that their minds remain flexible. They stay flexible as long as they start young. There's no hope of getting a good silversmith out of an art school—they come out with their ideas all set.'

To work exclusively from somebody's else's designs would not suit some silversmiths. But Stuart Devlin's craftsmen find that working for a large firm brings them security and freedom to do the work that they enjoy. Richard Cook, for instance, is Stuart Devlin's spoonmaker. He feels that if he were working on his own he would never be able to get the volume of work that Devlin gives him. He would be forced to extend his range of work and compromise his standards: also he would spend a fair proportion of his time on administration—something that he is spared at present.

Most silversmiths can hammer out or 'forge' a spoon, but Richard Cook is one of very few in London who do it all the time. The craftsman starts with a thin bar of silver which he heats on the forge. Heating the metal softens it, and makes it easier to hammer out. The first stage is hammering the silver bar to give a flat tip that will become the bowl of the spoon. Richard Cook uses a 10 lb. hammer and beats the silver against a smooth steel anvil. He reheats the silver at intervals to soften it. There is no margin for error. The heat applied to the silver must be just right or it will melt it. The force of the hammer must not be too great or the silver will crack.

To create the hollow of the bowl of the spoon a home-made tool called a 'stake' is used. This has a highly polished convex tip which will form the concavity of the bowl. Having heated the silver again he sets the flattened tip of the spoon on a metal slab which has a depression in it, and hammers the stake onto the silver, thus forcing it to take the shape of the stake. Next he sets the stake in the vice and holds the spoon onto it, beating the back of the spoon with a very light hammer to smooth out the silver. He gives the same attention to the handle, and now the spoon is ready for polishing. This is done on a lathe, using a series of different abrasives. Silver polishing is a highly skilled trade, and in the Devlin workshop it is carried out by separate craftsmen.

Stuart Devlin has his own showroom for his work, and most of it is sold from there. Like a fashion designer he has seasonal 'collections' when the new work is put on show. He also has exhibitions of his work abroad, including a highly successful one in the United Arab Emirates.

Badge and Insignia Maker

Chairmen of rural district councils, mayors of boroughs, heads of state, sportsmen, comedians, civil servants who have been decorated in the honours lists — all these have been the indirect clients of Jim Miller, badge and insignia maker. When a medal or badge is ordered from one of the large West End gold and silver shops, the chances are that Jim Miller or his assistants will be asked to do the job.

He is foreman of the insignia workshop at Padgett and Braham in Hackney, and one of very few craftsmen trained in this specialized trade.

'They call us the small makers. We're goldsmiths, not silversmiths. We don't touch hollow-ware.'

Starting from the simplest materials — flat sheets of silver and gold, and gold and silver wire, Jim Miller makes tiny, intricate pieces, using all the techniques available to the metalworker. The metal is bent into shape under heat, brazed (soldered), pierced (shapes cut out of the metal with a tiny fretsaw) drilled, and engraved. The silversmith's methods are here allied to the watchmaker's skill at assembling tiny parts. Making a badge for the Chairman of the Tiverton District Council, Jim Miller worked from a drawing provided by the College of Heralds, and cut and shaped the intricate heraldic devices from flat sheet metal. He prides himself on planning each piece so that it holds together like a watch, and does not need screws to hold the parts in place; a single pin through the middle is the only fastening that pride permits.

With medals, the basic shape is mass-produced. Sheet metal is pressed out with a die, but the details are put on by hand. The craftsman uses a flat-bladed engraving tool, the scorper, to create the flashing facets on a medal. On some insignia there are between 3,000 and 5,000 facets, all engraved by hand.

Jim Miller is cheerfully enthusiastic about his trade:

'We can make anything. If anyone can draw it, we can make it. We don't make money at this game compared with some of our friends like the miners. But we get a certain satisfaction from it. No one can push us around, because we are the only ones who know how long a job will take. The clients respect us—they come up and ask us how long we think we need; they don't come up here and tell us we're being too slow. We work better that way, it's a relaxed atmosphere.

You get blasé about the material you work with. Whether it's silver or gold, it's just metal to us. We don't put any less work into brass than we do gold. The clients get the same workmanship whatever metal they order. We do everything by hand. People have tried to take the handwork out of it, but this is one of the last trades that they can't modernize. Power cuts don't stop us. The only machines we use are electric drills—well, if those fail we still have these bow drills which work by hand.

We had a bumper period a few years back, when the GLC was formed. They made dozens of new Boroughs, and each one had to have a Mayoral badge. We get plenty of badges back for repair. They all sit round at their dinners flashing their badges and getting soup into them, and they send them back to us to be cleaned up. There's one Mayor who keeps dropping his badge and we get it back every six months or so.

You have to try and keep at maximum peak. If you feel that you could do better you're not doing well enough. All the same you're controlled by cost—and if the client doesn't want to pay too much, you have to sacrifice quality to speed. But with some jobs the client says he doesn't mind how much it costs and then you can make a really beautiful thing.'

As a fully qualified master goldsmith, Jim Miller is a Freeman of the Goldsmiths' Company and of the City of London. The recognition that the Establishment gives to craftsmen must contribute to their morale and to the high quality of their work.

Silver Engraver

Engraving is a separate craft within the silversmithing trade, and only a few silver-smiths do their own engraving. Engravers serve a five-year apprenticeship, and in that time they learn to do inscriptions, monograms and crests on presentation and commemorative silver, as well as more ambitious decorations.

The engraver cuts into the surface of a piece of silver with a sharp tool, removing a sliver of metal in the process. This distinguishes engraving from another form of surface decoration, chasing, in which a depression is created by hammering with a relatively blunt tool, a punch, into the silver, without removing any metal.

The skills of the silver engraver are much the same as those of the copperplate engraver, and they use the same tools; the scorper, with a blade of even thickness to cut even lines; and the graver, with a lozenged-shaped blade, that creates a thicker line when the craftsman presses deeper. Both types of tool have to be sharpened very often on a grinding stone. The craftsman tests them for sharpness on his thumbnail—you can always tell an engraver by the scratches on his nails.

It is the engraving itself that needs to show up on engraved silverware, not the printed image of it, as in copperplate work. So an additional tool, called a 'stitch', is used in this trade. The stitch has tiny grooves along the length of the blade, so that it creates a trough in the silver that is broken up by tiny ridges of metal; these catch the light and give the engraved line a bright, sparkling quality. The silver engraver also uses tools with curved handles, which enable him to get inside corners and hollows.

Most of London's engravers work in very small firms or one-man businesses, specializing in particular fields like clock-face engraving or trophy work. T. A. Wise of Hackney is one of the largest firms of engravers although they employ only seven men. They do an enormous range of work, from monograms on the handles of ivory hairbrushes, inscriptions on the inside of wedding-rings, to engraved pictures on cigarette boxes and carved and engraved decorations on ceremonial mace-heads. Their work has graced several palaces and many royal tables. Some of their customers come to them direct, but most of their work is done for the leading London gold and silver shops.

Enameller

The enameller paints with coloured glass. The pigments he uses are metallic oxides which are ground with powdered glass and water. The enameller paints this solution onto a metal foundation and then fires the work in a kiln. The glass melts and fuses onto the metal to form a hard, smooth, brilliantly coloured surface.

Any metal object can be enamelled. Snuffboxes, penknife handles, medals and insignia are the stock-in-trade of the traditional enameller. The most testing work is the painting of enamel miniatures: portraits or landscapes. This demands fine draughtsmanship and the most careful attention to technique. As in old master paintings, the colours are built up in transparent 'glazes'. The work is fired after each colour has been laid down and so the finished picture is built up in many stages. Each colour has to be freshly ground just before use. Stale colours form bubbles on the surface, and if these appear the work has to be scrapped.

The same processes, though more crude, are used to enamel domestic objects such as stoves, buckets and basins.

Teapot-handle Maker

For over sixty years, Jack Figgins has spent his working life making handles for silver teapots. He uses boxwood, ebony, and ivory, as well as a kind of compressed fibre material that comes in green, red and black. He works for the silversmiths Wakely and Wheeler and makes handles for all their silver pots as well as taking in work from outside. Over the years Mr Figgins has accumulated a large collection of templates of handle designs. Some of them he designed himself, and some are taken from antique handles.

For a particular pot Mr Figgins selects a suitable design and draws around the template onto his chosen piece of wood. He cuts out the rough shape with a bow saw and finishes it off with files and sandpaper. French polish gives the final lustre to the job.

'Fitting the handle to the pot is the main thing. It's the fit and getting it straight that are the difficult parts.

I was apprenticed in 1914. It took four years to learn, on and off. I ought to be retired now, but I'm carrying on because there's no one to take my place. I've had two boys here to learn the trade. One of them was doing very well, but then he left. He was very interested in golf, I think it was. Then I had another boy; he had toothache all the time, or so he said. He was away more time than he was here.

Most of the old ones are more reliable. They were made differently. Years ago when you had a job you had to stick tight. There was none of the moving around that there is these days. I think that the lads have too much of their own way. In the old days the parents were more strict. It didn't do us any harm. You can rely on us.

I used to be able to manage eight handles a day. Now I've slowed down and if I can do half of that number I'm pleased. I can still go on; I'm not finished yet. When you're working by hand you can see something you've made at the end of it; you can hold what you've made in your hand and admire it.'

As far as I know there is only one other craftsman making teapot-handles in London. This is W. E. Marshall, who is also an expert silver restorer.

PART IV

Woodworkers

There is a distinct polarization of the wood trades between the East and West Ends of London, though the rivalry between the two is not as bitter as it used to be. The West Enders were exclusively English craftsmen, serving strict apprenticeships, while the East Enders were largely immigrants, entering the trade more freely. The Brick Lane area of Shoreditch is still the centre of the East End trade, which specializes now in reproduction work.

Reproduction and restoration call for the skills of veneering, marquetry and woodcarving. These are aspects of the traditional cabinet-maker's craft. Modern furniture, which tends to dispense with these embellishments, is more allied to joinery, which is the craft of the assembly of solid woods.

Furniture Maker

In my view Richard la Trobe Bateman has made some of the most beautiful chairs that have been produced in this country since the war. His chairs have a kind of regal presence, a grandeur that is quite in contradiction to the simplicity of their making. What is more, they are comfortable. One of the design magazines did a survey of chairs by the top makers in the country, and Bateman's came out in the first three for comfort. All the same, to Bateman himself comfort is of secondary importance. Regarding the sometimes conflicting demands of beauty and function, he is quite clear where his priorities lie: 'If it came to the point that I could only achieve beauty and rhythm in a chair at the expense of comfort, I would sacrifice comfort every time.'

Bateman's furniture might be regarded as functional sculpture and in fact he was trained in sculpture and still teaches it part-time at a London art college. Here is an example of the new breed of artist-craftsmen who have emerged in this country since the war. Highly intelligent, articulate, and with an art college education in sculpture and furniture design that spanned eight years, Bateman was nearly thirty before he was ready to set up as a craftsman. But with all this training behind him he began working on his own, hardly knowing how to hold his tools. At college he and his fellow students had received a thorough training in design but had had very little practice in making the pieces that they had conceived on the drawing-board. Much of the physical work had been done for them by craftsmen employed as technicians. Richard la Trobe Bateman has his own views about the wastage record of art colleges:

'The art colleges have been producing furniture designers since the war. But where are they all? There are just about half a dozen of us working, and that's all. You know I have a theory about this—it's just my own cranky one I suppose—but I think that the class structure comes into this. I think that the technicians in art schools, who are working craftsmen themselves, are put off by the arrogant middle-class designers who are their students, and so they don't give away the secrets of their methods.

We've got to get away from the class conflict in the crafts. We've got to get away from the distinction between those that make and those that design. In Italy, I gather, they've got a very healthy relationship, especially in the hand-made car trade. There they have a long tradition of skill at panel-beating. And the panel-beaters are respected members of the community; there is no hierarchy from the designer down to the panel-beater; the value of each member of the team is equally respected. So they work together in a very healthy way.'

At present he works alone in a tiny basement room near Olympia. But with his name becoming established, Richard la Trobe Bateman is in the happy position of having orders for as much work again as he has already made in his whole working career. One commission is to design a whole room for one of the Cambridge colleges; tables, chairs, screen, light fittings, the lot. Inevitably he will need assistants, but he is determined to practise what he preaches; he will not perpetuate the hierarchy of the craftsman's workshop by creaming off all the design work himself, and farming out the work to skilled craftsmen to carry out. 'If I took on a couple of apprentices I would attach a lot of importance to their being involved with the creative side of the work.'

For Bateman the designing of a piece of furniture cannot be divorced from the activity of making it. He makes furniture like an artist might make a suite of drawings—they develop as he goes along. He makes chairs in series, and the fourth or fifth version is usually the definitive one that satisfies him.

For him the most successful works in any craft are those in which the quality is born out of the craftsman's ease and familiarity with his tools, which enables him to be true to the materials that he is using. He is inspired by the simple integrity of woodland crafts such as wattle-hurdling.

'The really attractive thing about it is the sureness of it, the inevitability. I want to get myself to the point where I can handle the materials quickly and strongly like that. I carved the number on the door of this house. But I was so slow and careful about it that it has none of the virility, the strength of the man who does it all the time and can knock it straight off.

In all the things that I do I want to develop the sureness of the man who has done nothing but that all his life. I want to be able to turn wood in that way, to cut wood with the draw knife, to cleave it like the woodcutter—not for clever crafty reasons, but because that way the quality of the material really comes across.'

With these ambitions he is very conscious of his lack of time, his technical shortcomings, and his own mortality.

'I have started so late and so far I have hardly any work to my name. At the moment my stuff is quite nice, that's all. If I keep going as I am, it's just a question of the design getting better. But I've got to do more, much more than that. I have the goal to do something that has weight, authority. If I'm lucky I might have thirty years. In thirty years' time I may be dead. That is my perspective.'

With such a fine body of work behind him in the first seven years of his career, and his extreme modesty about it, the next thirty years should see some very distinguished pieces coming from this craftsman's workshop.

Making riding breeches is a highly specialized kind of tailoring, and Mr Head of Newburgh Street, Soho, was the finest of his trade. But after sixty-six working years in Soho, Mr Head has now left London to start a new career making breeches for a Yorkshire firm.

The coppersmith and his forge. Copper vessels last a good deal longer than the craftsmen who make them. Until recently Mr Marchetti used to repair the pans that were made for Queen Victoria's coronation celebrations, but now his fire is extinguished, his workshop derelict, and Mr Marchetti, last of the line of an Italian firm of coppersmiths, has become another victim of London's blitz of property development.

Casting a bell at the Whitechapel bell foundry where bells have been made since 1570. Molten bell-metal, an alloy of copper and tin, is poured into the clay moulds. These bells are small fry compared with the thirteen tons of Big Ben, which was cast here on 10 April 1858. It is fitting that this firm, which cast the original Liberty bell for America, was commissioned to make small replicas of it for the bicentenary celebrations of 1976.

The lutemaker, Stephen Gottlieb, finishing an instrument. The bulbous body of a lute is built around a wooden framework, the mould. Here several moulds can be seen hanging neatly above the work-bench. Musical instrument makers tend to be the tidiest of craftsmen. They take pride in the display of their tools, many of which are home-made.

Chair Caner

It used to be fairly common to see a chair caner working outside on a London pavement, restoring the seats of chairs with cane or rush. But the itinerant caners have become scarce and the trade as a whole has dwindled to a handful of craftsmen. Not many modern chairs are caned, and the bulk of the work is done for the antique trade.

It takes a long time to cane a chair (fifteen hours or so for an ordinary seat and back panel) and there is a limit to the amount that can be charged for it. So caners often supplement their living in some other way. J. G. Parish is one of the top caners in London, but his main livelihood comes from running a little junk shop in Islington. He lives above the shop, and in a tiny room at the back he works until late at night restoring the cane seats of some exquisite antique chairs.

The chair caner needs very little space and few tools. He uses a sharp knife for cutting cane, a long needle or 'bodkin' for clearing the holes and manipulating the cane, and a set of wooden pegs to hold the cane in place in the holes.

The cane comes from the bark of a plant that used to be specially cultivated in the Far East. 'But now, after the trouble in Malaya and all those places, they don't cultivate it properly, but just collect it from the wild. It's like the difference between cultivated strawberries and the wild sort. The cane used to be like silk, but it comes all rough and knotted now. It holds me up, and it means I can't work as fast as I should.'

The first stage in caning a chair is to thread a line of canes between the front and back of the seat, and tie them into the holes in the frame. The craftsman has to judge the tension very carefully from the start. He wants the finished seat to be taut, but if the first canes are too tight it will become progressively harder to weave subsequent canes between them. When he reaches the end of a length of cane he trims it so that the loose ends are hidden under the frame of the chair; less meticulous craftsmen save cane by joining pieces together in the middle of the seat, a practice that looks shoddy and weakens the seat. Now a second set of canes, at right angles to the first, is woven in and out of the original row. With one hand on the vertical row Mr Parish plucks alternate canes like the strings of a guitar so that he can thread the horizontal canes through them at speed. Two diagonal rows of canes follow, at right angles to each other, and when the honeycomb pattern is complete, the pegs that wedge the canes in the holes are driven in tightly to make the seat secure. As a final decoration a 'beading' of cane is laid around the edge of the chair to cover the holes in the frame.

'I didn't serve an apprenticeship; I just fell into it. I went to work for a family—this trade used to run in families you know. I used to come home from school and sit down at it of an evening from 5.0 till 8.0. The old lady of the family was eighty-four when I joined them, and still working. They used to sit up all night long caning, the whole family of them. And they used to get 7½d a seat.

We used to do invalid chairs, and the old boats on the Thames always used to have canework at the back of the seats. There was a lot of canework on the *Titanic* too, you know. The doors were all done in double cane. The family I worked with had made the doors for the *Titanic,* and they were ever so upset when she went down.'

Mr Parish is a perfectionist, and he has the peace of mind of a man who knows that because of his shop he is not entirely dependent on his craft, and will not be jeopardized by thoroughness.

'The work has got to go into it and it takes time. You can't dodge it. But I must have it right. I've got into that way of life and there is no other way. Money has got nothing to do with it. If it costs me time to do it right, then it costs me, and that's all there is to it.'

Woodcarver

In the years of austerity during the war and shortly afterwards 'utility' was the byword in the furniture trade. Decoration was out. Carving was discouraged. The cabinet-makers could assist the war effort by making aircraft fuselages, but carvers were not wanted at all. To a man they drifted into other trades.

Consequently, there is a great shortage of carvers today, and they are much needed for restoration and reproduction work. One of the most versatile of the very few woodcarvers in the trade is David Shoolheifer, who works in Shoreditch. He can turn his hand to carved fireplaces as well as heraldic shields. He has carved the wooden fascia of a vintage Rolls-Royce, as well as the ball and claw feet on reproduction Jacobean chairs.

David Shoolheifer learnt the trade, somewhat unwillingly, from his father. 'I didn't go to art school. At first I didn't like it. But as you get better at a thing you become more deeply involved. Now sometimes when I'm working I lose all sense of time and I don't stop to eat and so on.'

At the beginning of a job he carves broad shapes with a large chisel and mallet, but as he gets to the finer details he uses smaller and smaller chisels and abandons the mallet.

'You feel your way as you carve and you try to improve the line of your work as you go along.'

His workbench is buried under rows of chisels with just a small clearing in the middle for him to work on. He is obsessed with tools. 'I've got all the chisels I need, but I still buy them if I go past a stall. I can't bear to see them sitting there going rusty.'

He rents his workshop very cheaply from the GLC, who built a large number of workshops for the craftsmen displaced in the redevelopment of the Shoreditch area. This is an inspired service more local councils would do well to follow.

Marquetry Maker

Marquetry is a hobby for thousands of people who produce pleasing pictures of country scenes, boats at sea, windmills and so on, out of tiny pieces of different kinds and colours of wood. But the professional marquetry experts are few and far between, and the trade has been much reduced since its hey-day in the eighteenth century.

The few remaining craftsmen in the trade are in great demand and one of the most versatile among them is Mr Dunn, who works from his home in Dollis Hill. He has made massive marquetry murals for ocean liners as well as the delicate traditional designs of flowers and fruit, shells and scrolls that are used to decorate the cases of clocks and barometers. He restores antique furniture that is inlaid with brass and mother-of-pearl as well as with wood marquetry. His is very much a family business. He learnt his skills from his father; his wife helps him; and his son is at present serving a seven-year apprenticeship under him. The Dunn family carry out all the processes of the trade in the cramped conservatory workshop of their home.

The raw materials for marquetry are veneers of many different kinds of wood. Some are natural colours and some stained. The craftsman selects his wood carefully, looking for interesting patterns or 'figures' in the wood grain. Wood that has been cut across the tree at a branch junction has a characteristic figure called the 'oyster', much used in marquetry. Wood from the yew tree is useful because it is marked with a soft, smoke-like figure which can have a good effect in murals.

As in so many trades, one of the greatest problems for the marquetry craftsman is getting hold of his materials. 'I use up to seventy different types of wood. It used to be possible to go in and choose a single leaf of veneer that you wanted. Then it came that you had to buy a whole bundle at a time. Now you just about have to buy up the whole stock for them to do business with you.'

The marquetry maker starts with an accurate master plan of the work to be done. He selects the range of woods that he will use and codes each type with a number. He marks up each section of the plan with the code number of the wood that will be used for it. Now he cuts up the plan with scissors, cutting roughly around each numbered piece. Each piece with a particular number is stuck down on the same piece of veneer. All the petals for a flower, for instance, may be made out of boxwood, and the cut-out paper shapes for the petals are all stuck down in such a way that the grain of the wood will point in the same direction in each one.

A second copy of the master plan is cut up and stuck down onto the wood that will be used for the background of the design.

Now the veneers, with the paper patterns stuck on, are ready for cutting. A single sheet of veneer would be too fragile and brittle to cut, and so it is backed with a piece of plywood, or else up to eight layers of the same veneer are stapled together and cut at the same time. This has the added advantage that eight identical designs can be cut out at once.

The craftsman does the cutting at a traditional chair called a marquetry-cutter's donkey. The chair is fitted with a fretsaw incorporating a device which ensures that the blade cuts horizontally all the time. The arm of the saw slides backwards and forwards on a bar, so that it cuts in one plane only; the slightest departure from the horizontal would mean that the pieces of veneer would not fit together when assembled. The veneers being cut are held in a vice which can be released by a pedal. The craftsman sits at the donkey, controlling the vice with his left foot, using his left hand to move the veneers through the angles to be cut, and working the saw with his right hand. Cutting all the pieces and the background for a complex floral design can take a whole day.

The mark of the professional shows up in the way that he finishes the separate pieces of wood. Not many amateurs know about the technique of 'shading', in which a three-dimensional effect can be created in the finished picture. This is done by dipping the edge of a cut piece of veneer into a pan of hot sand. The sand singes the wood slightly, and darkens it, giving the appearance of shadow.

Now comes the assembly. The pieces are laid out on a board and fitted together like a jigsaw puzzle. When the design is assembled the craftsman mixes a little boxwood sawdust with carpenter's glue and wipes the mixture over the surface, pressing it into the spaces between the pieces. This is enough to hold them together. The whole work is flattened overnight between boards and this is the end of the job. It is now the cabinet-maker's task to apply the marquetry design to a piece of furniture, and to polish it, just like any other piece of veneer.

French Polisher

In simple terms French polishing is a matter of rubbing layer upon layer of white polish into the surface of a piece of furniture, smoothing down with sandpaper between layers and polishing it up with a cloth until the final result is a mirror-smooth surface in which the colour and the figure of the wood are brought up to their best advantage.

In practice the trade of French polishing is far more involved than this. The polisher can manipulate the colour of the wood as he goes along. He removes colour by bleaching, and adds colour by using tinted polishes and stains. He hides the junctions between separate pieces of wood by staining them so that the colours match, and even by painting the grain pattern of one piece of wood so that it extends into the other.

Ernest Crook polishes barometer and clock-cases for Bill Marney's firm of barometer makers. He is talking of retiring soon, and there is no one to replace him:

'The Victorians liked their mahogany to be a plum colour with plenty of red in it. But going back to the eighteenth century they wanted mahogany to be brown. You see this one? It's too red, but a bit of blue in the white polish will tone it right down.

The first polish is called a wash-in. It drops into the wood and after half an hour you wouldn't know it was there. If I want to change the colour I use a water stain and wash the stain in with polish; that fixes it. You thin the polish with white oil; it acts as a lubricant. Sandpaper again. I do this again and again until all the grain in the wood is filled up. Then I look at it and say that's ready to finish. I sandpaper again until there are no lines on the surface. Oil and polish. Oil and polish. When I'm working, everything's done automatically; how can you explain what you do? If I want it to go a bit darker I use button polish. I make up a colour from spirits, black polish and red polish; I can put figure into a piece of wood using this. There's nothing clever about it; it's just experience. That's when the skill comes in — after years of experience.

We've had lots of young lads here to learn the trade. But it's hard to find a lad that's interested; the environment is wrong. Kids like to be with kids. I don't think that's always a good thing — they play up when they're all together. You've got to be gentle with young people; they take offence easily. So I talk to them in a fatherly way. It takes all my time but if I've got a bright lad it's worthwhile. You can't pick them off trees you know. And the trouble is that once you've found a good lad and taught him the basics, he's ready to make a move.

The only polishers around are about my own age. Once my generation goes, that will be it.'

There is no real short cut to the superb finish that can be achieved by a craftsman polishing by hand for hours on end. There is a spray that can be used to give a cheap and glossy alternative to French polish, but it is a very poor substitute for the real thing.

Barrow Maker

There is nobody quite like the street traders or 'costermongers' of London and there is nothing quite like the barrows they use either. These barrows are unique to London and they have evolved gradually over the years to suit the changing needs of the street traders. Costermongers' barrows used to be fitted with shafts so that they could be drawn by donkeys. The shafts have evolved into handles so that a man can push his barrow on the daily journeys between the garages where the barrows are stored overnight and the street pitch where the costermonger carries out his trade.

Market barrows are never sold, but are hired out by the firms that make them. Each maker has his own mark which he carves on all his barrows for recognition. He also carves his name on every barrow in a traditional flowing script which is unique to the barrow trade, but is also reminiscent of the lettering used on gipsy caravans and on the traditional narrow boats.

Although the fruit and vegetable market has moved away from Covent Garden the oldest firm of barrow makers in London, Ellen Keeley of Neal Street, still does a flourishing business. The Keeleys are a close-knit family firm that has survived for four generations by changing with the times. They started up as makers of horse-carts and vehicles. Horses began to go out and there was a demand for mobile market barrows, so they moved into barrows. Now the barrow trade has gone down a bit and so the Keeley firm does more and more work on props for television and film companies.

Keeley's is run by two cousins, Terry O'Doherty and Johnny Sullivan, both of them great-grandsons of Ellen Keeley who started the firm. Terry O'Doherty spends most of his time outside the workshop, collecting rents for barrows from the street traders, and organizing the TV hire service, but he has not lost the knack of carving the old barrow maker's script. He places a flat piece of wood in a vice, marks it with two parallel lines and, without any preliminary drawing, begins to tap a V-shaped chisel into the wood. In three minutes flat he has carved 'Ellen Keeley on hire' in beautiful flowing letters, perfectly formed and spaced.

'I could carve these letters before I could write. You can only do the words that you know straight off. New words you have to practise. I'm not so good at it now; we don't often have to do it. But the old boys like Johnny's father used to do it every day and they had an exquisite style. Someone asked him to do the alphabet once. He could do the lot straight off except for the x and the z. He had a problem with those two. You can tell who cut a sign anywhere. Here, this is one of mine. That one is Johnny's father's.

This is softwood and it's not as good as ash. You can get a level depth with ash, and the chisel doesn't need to be so sharp. It's absolutely unique, this barrow maker's lettering. People have written theses about it, but nobody has discovered where it originated.

There was a bloke on the council who wanted to make all barrows the same. He wanted to bring in plastic barrows—he really believed in it. He wanted them to be like matchboxes, fitting together all neat-like. That's when I saw trouble brewing for the business, and I moved into the film trade, making props and such.'

The new Covent Garden market is a councillor's dream because there are hardly any barrows used there. But Keeley's do not mind, because, like many a grander company, they have practised the policy of 'diversification'.

Brushmaker

Brushmaking is an ancient but rapidly declining trade. More brushes are made now than ever before, but most of them by machine. It takes a man twenty minutes to make an ordinary domestic broom by hand, but a machine can turn out 600 in an hour. All the same, hand-made brushes are still in demand because they are much longer-lasting than machine-made ones and they can be individually made for special uses. There is no machine, for instance, that can make the brooms, six feet wide, that are used to create the light and dark stripes on the grass at Tottenham Hotspur football ground. These are made by Mr Ogilvie of J. Hoolahan & Co in Southwark.

Only just short of eighty, Mr Ogilvie is one of the last of the old school of 'pan-hands'. This is the trade term for the traditional brush-workers who sit round the pan of boiling pitch which they use to secure the bristles in the brush heads.

The head of a brush is cut from a block of beech or ash. Holes are drilled for the bristles, and there now follows the almost ritualistic process of filling the brush heads. The pan-hand sits facing his pan of steaming pitch. On his left he has a pile of bristles, and a second pile consisting of six-inch lengths of hemp twine. With his left hand he picks up a fistful of bristles and taps them so that they all settle to the same length. With his right hand he takes just the right number for one knot and fans them out with his thumb. Now he dips the fanned tips into the pitch. In his left hand he has a piece of twine ready and he binds this around the tips of the bristles and tucks it underneath. The twine is saturated in pitch and binds the bristles tightly. Now he dips the tip of the whole knot into the pitch again, and presses it into the hole in the brush head. As the pitch cools down it hardens and makes the knot firm and permanent.

Speed is at a premium in this trade. Brushmakers used to do piecework and were paid according to the number of knots that they made. Mr Ogilvie's list of prices, dating from 1916, records that brushmakers were paid one penny for every seventeen knots of a broom. For beehive boot wipers, chimney-sweep block heads, golf-course brooms, the rates were nine, twelve and fifteen knots to the penny respectively.

Cooper

The cooper makes casks and barrels. Sadly this most ancient and skilled trade has been declining steadily in London since the turn of the century. Brewers have moved over to metal casks, and wine firms ship their products in fibreglass containers. In 1901 there were about three thousand coopers at work in London. Now there are only a few dozen.

A barrel is made out of staves of hardwood tapered at each end, bent by heat, and held together by hoops of steel. Not only must the cooper make every seam watertight, but he has to build the barrel to hold a required volume of liquid. This achievement is even more remarkable when one considers that the cooper judges everything by eye and seldom takes a measurement. As well as a sensitive eye the cooper needs immense stamina and strength. He is working with hardwood and fashioning it by hand. The whole cask is held together by the pressure of the hoops which are hammered into place with sheer strength.

Within the coopering trade there is a friendly rivalry between two factions, the brewers' coopers and the wine and spirit men. At trade fairs the two parties used to gather at opposite sides of the hall and not mix together. The brewers' cooper regards himself as a cut above the wine man. Marginally more skill is needed in making a beer cask, because it has to be made to hold an accurate volume, to the nearest pint; there is a little more leeway with a wine barrel. Also the brewers' cooper has to shave the inside of a beer barrel until it is absolutely smooth, because the cracks and crannies in the wood can harbour bacteria which make the beer go off. This is not necessary with wine casks. Brewers' coopers' foremen used to test the smoothness of a barrel by running a silk handkerchief around the inside. If the silk caught on a splinter, the cooper had to shave the barrel again.

Tom Wood is a cooper with Young's Brewery in Wandsworth. He is a superb craftsman, but he has been shadowed by the decline of his trade: he was made redundant five times before joining Young's. Most of his time is spent on repair work, but at weekends he keeps his eye in at making barrels by helping at a firm of wine and spirit coopers in Kingston. He reckons to turn out three new barrels on a good day.

A beer barrel will last fifty years if it is well maintained. To replace a damaged stave, Tom Wood knocks the barrel apart, cuts a new stave to the correct size, and puts the barrel together again. There are several machines that help with the work, but Tom Wood does most things by hand.

To make a stave, the cooper starts with an even length of straight-grained oak. (The best wood for coopering is Memel oak from Russia, which is seldom available now). He cuts the taper at each end with an axe. The cooper's axe is a heavy and unwieldy instrument, reminiscent of an executioner's weapon; its handle is offset from the line of the blade, so that the cooper does not graze his knuckles against the stave. Tom Wood handles it with astonishing skill, shaving off small slivers of wood with each blow so that the final result is a smooth, even taper.

Next the stave has to be planed along each edge to form a bevel so that it will fit against its neighbours without any gaps between them. For this, the cooper uses the jointer, which is an enormous plane about six feet long. It is set up on the floor, blade uppermost, with one end resting on a trestle. The cooper fashions the joint of the stave by sliding it over the stationary blade, holding the stave at the correct angle to produce the bevel.

Next the stave has to be hollowed out on the inside with a rounded drawknife. This is a double-handled knife that is worked by drawing it towards the body. Now the wood has to be bent with heat, to give it the required curve. In repair work the new stave is usually steamed so that it can be bent to shape, but when making a new barrel the cooper first sets up all the staves in position with a couple of ash-wood hoops to hold them together. This is called 'raising' the barrel. Now he lights a fire of wood shavings in a small brazier called a cresset and sets the barrel over it. When the staves are hot they can be bent without splitting, and the cooper does this by banging the steel hoops into position, thus forcing the tapered ends of the staves to come together.

Shaving the inside of the barrel follows. A painful job this, because it is difficult for the cooper to avoid rasping his forearms on the lip of the barrel. A groove is cut at the top to take the head of the cask. This is done with a curved plane, which is pulled around the lip of the cask. To make an absolutely watertight seal a few reeds are used to caulk the joint between the head and the body of the barrel. Now the cask is good for many years' service before it will need to come back for repair.

One of the coopers' perks is a free supply of beer provided by the brewery, though Tom Wood has usually sweated out his ration by lunchtime. Wine and spirit coopers have their own effective, if illegal, way of getting a supply of liquor—by steaming it out of the woodwork of the barrels. When a freshly emptied rum or whisky cask came into the workshops, the coopers used to boil up a gallon of water, pour it into the cask, shake it up a bit, and leave it for a couple of days. The powerful liquor that resulted was called 'bull'. The coopers at the dock used to pilfer a little liquor from the casks by putting a straw through a gimlet hole and sucking up a few gulps; this was called 'sucking the monkey'. Another expression, 'tap the admiral' stems from the legend in the coopers' trade that Nelson's body was brought back from Trafalgar preserved in a cask of rum, but when the barrel was opened it was found to be dry. The dead admiral's high spirits had mysteriously passed to the sailors and coopers on the voyage home.

PART V

Musical instrument makers

The standard of musical education in schools is constantly improving. School-leavers have a better knowledge of music than ever before. The pleasant results of this have filtered through to the instrument makers, who are enjoying a boom. The high general level of knowledge and appreciation has another effect too. The customers know a good instrument when they hear one, and their discernment keeps the standard of instrument-making high.

Concertina Maker

The concertina is one of the very few truly English instruments. It was invented by the English physicist, Sir Charles Wheatstone, in 1829 and in 1848 a firm was started by John Crabb in Islington to make concertinas for the inventor. Several concertina-makers have come and gone since then, but the Crabb firm is still going strong. They are now the only concertina makers left in the country and they have a long waiting list of customers all over the world. Between them the four men at Crabb's make about a hundred new concertinas in a year, and restore about three hundred old ones.

Concertinas are the Crabb family's life. During the day, Harry Crabb and his son Derek make instruments. In the evenings they play them and teach others to play. They are self-contained in their world of concertinas and music. In the quiet atmosphere of their workshop the Crabbs seem to be detached from the nagging issues of our time.

'We run this business as a sort of hobby. We get deep satisfaction from making the instruments. You make one and when you hear the music coming out it's a joy. We've never really had enough money. We just happen to like making beautiful concertinas.

There are 1,500 parts in a concertina and we make them all. We make one part at a time, in batches. There are four of us here and we take turns to do different things.

Concertinas began to die out in the 1920s when the piano accordion came on the market; these are much easier to play of course. After the war, demand fell to zero. But we went on making concertinas, because we always had faith that they would come back. And now we have a three-year waiting list. There's a fellow in New York who wants to order batches of five hundred concertinas at a time. We tell him that each order will take us twenty-five years to complete.

We like to sell them at a price that the people who are going to play them can afford. We want the instrument to be played. Sometimes a person buys an instrument in a junk shop for £30 and he reckons he has a bargain. He brings it to us and we tell him that it's no good. He realizes that he has been duped and he wants to get his money back. So he sells it to someone else for a bit more. That way an instrument goes the rounds and it prevents people playing. So now we usually buy them up when people bring them here. They're no use to us but it prevents a useless instrument putting people off.'

The Crabbs still carried on when their business went through a bad patch in the 1930s. Equally they are quite unaffected by their present boom. They just continue to do what they enjoy doing most—making concertinas.

51

Violin Maker

To get the best sound, the violin maker has to select his woods with extraordinary care. The belly of the instrument is made from white pine, and the purists specify that the pine should be Swiss and that it should be cut not only from a tree on the south side of the forest, but also from wood on the south side of the tree. Such wood has been exposed to the greatest amount of sunlight and will have the closest and straightest grain. Some experts have even gone so far as to say that the wood must come from a certain distance between the bark and the heart of the tree, and between the boughs and root.

The choice of wood is only one example of the refinements that are attached to each process of this craft. The violin took its present shape in the sixteenth century, and in the intervening years there have been surprisingly few modifications to the basic design and methods of construction. Each process has been tried and proved by generations of craftsmen. Such is the sensitivity of the violin that only the most subtle refinements distinguish the work of the greatest makers from that of their lesser brethren. Even such a seemingly minor factor as the composition of the final varnish has a strong influence on the tone of the instrument.

One of the tests of the violin-maker's skill is the shaping of the belly and the back of the instrument. The rounded contour of these parts is made not by bending a flat piece of wood, but by carving out the correct shape from a solid. To make a violin belly, a wedge of wood is split in two and the two halves glued together along the middle. Since the two halves come from the same wedge, the grain of the wood matches and the pattern or figure of the belly is symmetrical. The craftsman cuts out the characteristic outline of the belly with a bow saw, and then hollows out the wood with gouges and a violin plane (a small brass plane with an oval blade). As he works he tests the thickness of the wood with calipers. The wood of the belly has to be thicker in areas of greater tension and the thickness also has to be adjusted according to the hardness of the wood. If the wood is too thin, the tone of the fiddle is weak; if too thick, the instrument sounds heavy and dull.

Paul Voigt works on his own in one small room just off Gerrard Place in Soho. He comes from a great family of violin makers, stretching back in an unbroken line to 1690. Beside his bench he keeps a miniature violin, six inches long and a perfect working model, which he made as his masterpiece on graduation from the Mittenwald violin school in Bavaria. Paul Voigt specializes in repairing instruments, and as he has violins of all periods passing through his hands, he is well qualified to make an assessment of modern craftsmen:

'The standard of work is very good as far as craftsmanship goes. But the individualist has gone. Now we live in a machine age and although instruments are made by hand, the modern craftsman strives for a machine-like accuracy.

Modern violins are beautifully made but they all have this precision. You could call it a photographic quality. They all become the same, and that's boring.

With the old Italian makers—there were several of them here in Soho—you got the impression that they got a bit of wood and carved it and the shape grew out of it. So it really was a handmade thing. When they carved the scroll, the two sides might have been quite different—but it had character.

Soho and St Paul's churchyard used to be the violin-making centres of London. But of all the single makers in Soho I'm the only one left. They used to be tucked away in attics and little rooms all over the place.

There was a friendly competition between us. Take the violin bridge for instance . . . we could see a bridge made by another craftsman, and we would say "That's very nice but I think I could do better." That's the kind of competition that keeps your standards up.'

Paul Voigt does repairs mainly for professional orchestral players, but he also gets work from an unexpected quarter:

'Nowadays the group boys come into the picture. They have special bridges on their violins and they amplify the sound. I had one of them come in here: "How much are violin bows?" "Six pounds," I say. "I'll have half a dozen," he says. Well now, a violin bow will normally last three years, but they use metal strings, so they get through them. A few weeks later he came back: "I'll have a dozen bows," he says, "We're going to America." When they got there I received a cable: "Send a dozen more." So when I saw him again I asked him what he did with them. It turned out that they were using them like bows and arrows to flick cards out into the audience.'

Paul Voigt's workroom is a quiet haven in a particularly frenzied part of Soho. He likes to listen to the comments of the revellers as they pass his window.

People think that the violin maker is an extinct animal. I hear people going by outside, and one fellow said "Cor, look . . . a violin maker." And the other fellow said: "He must be a right sucker." People often say to me how nice it must be to be your own boss and free. But it's not like that. When the door's closed there's nothing coming in.'

Lute Maker

The surge of interest in early music has created a new demand for craftsmen to create instruments to play it on. Early stringed instruments such as lutes, citterns, viols and rebecks; keyboard instruments like clavichords and harpsichords, virginals and spinets; and wind instruments like krummhorns and serpents; these are all being made in increasing numbers by a growing band of young craftsmen, professionals and hobbyists. Their skills range from the brilliant to the very bad, but they share a passion for the sound of a music that had been almost totally forgotten until quite recently.

There are huge problems attached to the making of early instruments. There is no continuous tradition of making them; the skills and methods have been lost and they have to be invented anew by each craftsman for himself. So the maker of early instruments is more free than, say, a violin maker, to develop his own methods, but equally he is more liable to make mistakes.

The only way to create an authentic instrument is by studying original examples that are preserved in museums and collections. Ideally the craftsman needs to take an instrument to pieces to see how it is constructed, but the custodians of these treasures are not too keen on this. Most craftsmen have to content themselves with taking external measurements and with playing the original instrument to assess the 'authentic sound'.

Authenticity of sound is itself a knotty problem. Naturally the later instruments are the best preserved; the earlier ones are often damaged, and some were adapted or improved for later use. Also many of the earliest instruments have built-in faults that were ironed out in later developments. Should the modern maker reproduce the original instrument, faults and all, or should he incorporate the later improvements? This question is the subject of endless debate. Some years ago it was the custom to improve upon the original instruments, to 'update' them in the light of later knowledge. Now many musicians feel that instruments should be as nearly as possible contemporary with the music that is to be played on them. Players are demanding exact replicas of specific instruments.

Stephen Gottlieb is a young Clerkenwell craftsman who made his first lute because he wanted a suitable instrument to play himself. He became involved, and now after only a few years he has established himself as one of the most respected lute makers in the country.

The lute is one of the most difficult instruments to make, as well as being one of the hardest to play. The body of the instrument has a flat soundboard and a pear-shaped back. At least five different kinds of wood go into a lute: sycamore for the back, pine for the soundboard, ebony or rosewood for the finger-board, beech for the bridge and boxwood for the tuning pegs. Making the body of the lute is like a refined version of coopering. Barrels and lutes are both made with tapering pieces

A characteristic silver goblet by Stuart Devlin. The bowl of the goblet was raised from a flat sheet of silver and the hammer marks have been retained as a feature. Raising, which is done by hammering the silver against steel stakes is one of the highest skills of silversmithing. The stem of this goblet was cast in a mould from a carved original.

Bert Kensley is an insignia maker with Padgett and Braham in Hackney. Here he is demonstrating a pump drill to pierce a hole in silver. This highly effective type of drill has been in use for thousands of years – a version was used by the ancient Greeks. The basic shapes of insignia like these CBEs are punched out by machine, but the craftsman engraves the many facets on each by hand.

Organ pipes are made from an alloy of tin and lead. The percentages are varied to change the timbre. Here Mr Noterman, who builds organs in Shepherds Bush, arranges his pipes in sequence. There are about three thousand in this organ.

of wood, cut so that they fit flush together. The lute maker builds up the body of the lute on a wooden framework called the mould, bending the ribs over the mould and gluing them at the edges. Stephen Gottlieb built his own moulds from measurements taken from early lutes.

He takes enormous care with the finish of his instruments, scraping and sanding the wood for days until it is perfectly smooth.

'You can't divorce the appearance of an instrument from the sound. The look and feel of an instrument are really important to the player; it's all part of the aesthetics of the thing. It's a unity. The sound and the appearance are one.

A student came here once to watch me work—he wanted to write a thesis on lute-making. Well, he sat here the whole morning, and the only thing I did in that time was scrape down one piece of wood. He must have found it really boring because he didn't come back again. People think that the crafts are glamorous. In fact the moments of excitement are very few and far between.

The essence of making an instrument is to know what a player needs. I don't think that I could make an instrument if I didn't know what it was like to play one.

A lot of people started making lutes after buying a lute kit; it's the old English amateur approach to things. In Germany you have to have a formal education before you are allowed to make a living at a craft and employ people. Here anyone can set up as a craftsman and the only way that standards are maintained is by the clients' buying only what is best.'

All Stephen Gottlieb's instruments are made to order for musicians who know exactly what they want. But he is beginning to feel that he would like to start making his instruments as he thinks they should be. 'I think perhaps that the maker sometimes reaches a point where he knows better than the musician how the instrument should be. The answer is that you work at the old techniques until you know all about it. There's a lot to be said for doing what the great masters did, until you reach a complete understanding.'

In this respect he is following a well-tried path; even Stradivarius worked for many years on conventional violins before he was ready to introduce his own refinements.

Piano Maker

In February 1818 Beethoven wrote to a London piano-maker, Thomas Broadwood, enthusiastically accepting the gift of a grand piano: 'I shall regard it as an altar upon which I will place the choicest offerings of my mind to the divine Apollo.'

Liszt was more practical about the Broadway pianos: 'No pianoforte lasts anything like so well as those of Broadwood.' Liszt's recommendation was put to the test when in 1904 a Broadwood piano was taken with Scott to the Antarctic.

The Broadwood firm itself has proved as durable as its pianofortes. The original John Broadwood launched his piano in 1771, sixty-odd years after the instrument had been invented. In the 1970s the Broadwood family are still running the firm. Over the years they have introduced refinements that have become standard fittings on all pianos; they were the first to fit pedals, for instance. And they led the field in design: some of the early Broadwood cases were made to Sheraton's designs. Later they were associated with William Morris's arts and crafts movement, and Burne-Jones designed and painted several of their pianos.

The Broadwood piano works occupies a spacious factory on an industrial estate in Acton. Fifteen craftsmen make up the team and between them they turn out five pianos a week. Demand for their pianos exceeds production and there is an eighteen-month waiting list. They have two types of grand piano in production at present and two uprights, though they are constantly developing new models.

The heart of the piano is the sound-board, a gently curving expanse of wood that amplifies the vibrations of the strings. The strings are stretched on a sturdy iron frame, which has to withstand a tension of some twenty tons. The strings pass over a curving piece of wood, the bridge, which transmits their vibrations to the sound-board. The most delicate processes in piano-making are the construction of the sound-board and the hand-carving of the bridge. At Broadwood's these operations are carried out by a craftsman of long experience, Ron Mickish, whose father did the same work before him.

'My father used to say "Get that done" and so I'd watch people and see how they did it and then I'd do it myself. That's the way to learn. You come to tell a good sound-board just by the look of it. It is supposed to form a section of an enormous sphere. There's a pressure of half a ton on the sound-board so everything has to be made right.'

The sound-board is made up of parallel strips of wood, glued together and reinforced at the back with eleven supporting bars. The wood is Canadian spruce and each piece has to be cut with the grain going a particular way to give the maximum strength. The best wood has seventeen annual rings to the inch. When glueing the sections of the sound-board Ron Mickish used the traditional piano maker's method of pressing down on the wood. Supple rods of lance-wood, called 'go-bars', are bent, and one end placed against the sound-board, the other end against a firm wooden ceiling. The tension in the bent wood provides the correct pressure.

The bridge is made of white beechwood and Ron Mickish carves it by hand. He never uses a mallet, but hits the head of the chisel with the palm of his hand. He claims that he can control the cut much better that way.

The piano cases are made at the Acton factory by the Broadwood cabinet-makers, but the construction of the mechanical parts, the 'action' of the piano, is a separate trade and is carried out by an independent firm.

A total of 180 hours' work goes into an upright piano and 200 hours into a grand. This provides an illuminating contrast with a statistic in the *Guinness Book of Records* which states that the record for demolishing an upright piano and passing the entire wreckage through a circle nine inches in diameter is two minutes twenty-six seconds, and was achieved by a team of six men representing Ireland in 1968.

Organ Builder

'Ah, so you want to talk about this trade. How many days can you spare?' This is Mr Noterman talking, the presiding genius of a small firm of church organ-builders in a quiet backstreet in Shepherd's Bush.

'People don't understand what's involved in this trade. You tell someone that there are three thousand pipes in a small organ and it doesn't mean much to them. But show them an organ set up in a church and show them the rows of pipes all set up on their chests with gangways between them for access and you can see their jaws drop.'

The modern organ is the end-product of several thousand years of evolution. It all started with simple wind instruments: flutes, whistles and the like. The ancient Chinese set a score of pipes on a wind-chest which the player filled with air by blowing through a mouthpiece. The Romans took the principle a stage further by supplying air to the pipes through hand-operated leather bellows, on the principle of bagpipes. The bellows idea meant that the strength of more than one man could be used to produce wind. By the tenth century the organ could already make a thunderous sound. The instrument at Winchester Cathedral was described by the contemporary monk Wulstan:

'Twice six bellows above are ranged in a row and fourteen lie below. These by alternate blasts supply an immense quantity of wind and are worked by seventy strong men, labouring with their arms, covered with perspiration, each one inciting his companions to drive the wind with all his strength that the full-bossomed box may speak with 400 pipes which the hand of the organist governs . . . Like thunder the iron tones batter the ear so that it may receive no sound but that alone. The music is heard throughout the town and the flying fame therof is gone out over the whole country.'

The modern organ still has the same basic elements as its tenth-century ancestor in Winchester—a bellow to produce wind (electric now), a chest which acts as a wind reservoir and a range of pipes that produce the notes. But the sophistication of the modern instrument is such that the organ-builder needs to have dozens of different skills at his fingertips. He has to know about air currents and velocities so that he can get his wind supply right; he has to be able to build complex electrical circuits linking the keyboard to the pipes. Musically he is like the conductor of a gigantic symphony orchestra. Each pipe has to be regulated and tuned like a separate instrument and each one has to sound harmonious with the others. He needs to have an equal facility for wood and metal-work. In short the organ-builder is a universal craftsman, and not surprisingly this kind of superman is a rare breed.

Among the six craftsmen that he employs, Mr Noterman is lucky to have a young nephew who is infected with his own passion for the work:

'He's been bitten by the trade, like me. Unless you're bitten hard by the bug you won't get on. You don't go into this for commercial reasons. But you come to get a feeling for the work and so you stick with it.

You learn the trade by serving an apprenticeship, but the organ builder can't know all the trade by the end of it. Between the ages of thirty-five and foty-five you should be in your top form and from that point on you use the knowledge that you've acquired. If you lived to be a hundred and twenty you'd have accumulated so much knowledge about organ-building that your head would burst. Things that you're not using every day get pushed into the background of your mind, and you only dredge them out when the need arises.

The craftsmen who entered this trade at the turn of the century had the intelligence of people who are now streamed into universities and technical colleges. These people don't go into the crafts any more. There's a kind of stigma attached to making things with your hands. So the young people we get tend not to have the IQ to enable them to hold all the knowledge in their heads.

One thing you have to do is to build an organ to suit a particular church. If an organ's at the back or hidden in a side aisle, or if there's plenty of wood about muffling the sound, then you need to build more weight into it. You get to know these things so you don't have to think about them; they become automatic.

We make organs for all the Christian sects. If it's for an Anglo-Catholic Church you have to make a more musical instrument than for the "low" Church.

You have to alter your style to suit the ritual. The Anglo-Catholics have the most musical ritual, which may have something to do with the fact that they were always the moneyed people.'

In the 1920s and 1930s many cinema organs were made, which brought a lot of money into the trade. But now the Church is the only patron for the conventional organ and, as everyone knows, the Church is hard up. What is more, the furnishing of the church, which includes the organ, has to be met by the contributions of the shrinking congregations.

Little wonder that a trade that employed some 2,500 craftsmen at the turn of the century has been reduced to about a tenth of that figure. The number of organ-building firms in the country has dwindled to under a dozen.

Fairground-organ Maker

Victor Chiappa is a third-generation maker of fairground-organs and the last of his line. He makes and repairs the automatic organs that play tunes from perforated cardboard rolls. One of Victor Chiappa's main lines of business is making the music rolls for his customers. He has the patterns for over 2,000 tunes, many of them the real old favourites going back sixty years and more. But he can still make tunes from modern songs. If a customer wants to play the top of the pops on a fairground organ, Victor Chiappa can oblige. A friend arranges the music for the organ and makes a master stencil, and Mr Chiappa cuts the music himself, using a nineteenth-century perforating machine of his grandfather's that is still in perfect working order.

Mr Chiappa is seventy-five, works alone, and has nobody to follow on from him:

'My son wouldn't join this trade; he can do better for himself. I used to have a couple of women here punching cards, but they were taken ill and I lost them.

I'm at retiring age and so I don't have to work. But I keep on working because I enjoy it. I do it all myself. I don't mind cutting the tunes; it gives me a chance to sit down.

The young people these days want something for nothing. I'd like to see them do some of the hours that I do. I go out for three or four days at a time to do a repair job for a customer. I've just come back from Devon. If my customers are in a bit of trouble I help them—that's all there is to it. Well, this time I asked the customer to help me a bit; you know, turn this screw, hold that and so on. And they're not soppy, those showmen, but by the end of the day he was worn out. He said he thought I was going to tire him out. That's my way. I'll work from eight in the morning till eleven at night to get the job done for a customer if he's in a corner.'

Mr Chiappa is one of the original makers. He has spent his lifetime making and installing automatic organs for the original sites, the fairgrounds. Meanwhile these instruments have become collectors' pieces and have been taken up by enthusiasts who are not showmen. The next generation of craftsmen, the restorers, will come from the ranks of these enthusiasts. The natural progression of the trades has speeded up so much that the restorers start work before the original makers have put down their tools.

Musical-box Restorer

The best musical boxes were made in France and Switzerland in the nineteenth century. They have elaborate brass movements worked by powerful springs and they are usually mounted in beautiful carved and inlaid cases.

Keith Harding's firm specializes in restoring musical boxes and mechanical dolls. With a science degree, a training in clockmaking, and a passionate feeling for music, Keith Harding is the epitome of a new breed of craftsmen. He is eclectic, articulate, efficient and a sound businessman. His employees are all young, keen and well paid. His workshop is like a research laboratory, clean, well-lit and fitted up with all the latest engineering gadgetry. Keith Harding seems to be inventing the tools and techniques of his trade as he goes along, which is paradoxical since he is working exclusively on antique instruments. The original makers of musical boxes must have come across the same problems that he does, but he has found new ways to solve them. When the pins on the cylinder of a box are bent, he straightens them with a hypodermic needle. When he needs to put down an even layer of glue on the inside of a brass cylinder he has developed a technique using a lathe and a red-hot poker. He spins the cylinder on the lathe and holds the poker inside it. The heat dissolves the glue and the centrifugal force distributes it evenly. Keith Harding is even toying with the idea of generating his own electricity from the energy of the sun.

'Everyone talks about the vanishing crafts. People seem to be nostalgic for the old. But what really matters are the living crafts. There's nothing really very romantic about the idea of a craftsman in his garret, doing his work for nothing and being exploited on all sides. The craftsmen who work like that are just inefficient and they deserve to go out of business.

I started out fourteen years ago. Then, Clerkenwell was right down. The craftsmen were giving up and going out of business. Everyone had their trade secrets. Nobody helped anyone else. And they used to tell me that it was no good doing quality work. It had to be cheap to sell. But I went against this and set up to sell quality. And I charge a proper price for it.

I had to persuade craftsmen to accept proper pay. I used to take work to an old clockmaker called Osborn. Old Osborn would have gone bust years before if I hadn't given him double what he asked.

We share our knowledge in this firm; we don't have any trade secrets. We publish a workshop manual so that anyone can follow the processes that we use. We're not afraid of anyone pinching our work—there's plenty of work for anyone who is capable of it. And we know that if anyone uses our ideas they will be five years out of date, because we will have moved on to new ideas.

There are some craftsmen who are a bit easy on the ethics of their trade. I've seen a craftsman produce a perfect reproduction of an eighteenth-century clock. And the craftsman was justly proud of it. But he didn't feel responsible for what the client did with it. And the client took it round to an engraver and had the name of the original maker engraved on it. So the craftsman's work became nothing more than a forgery, instead of the splendid achievement that it was.'

The musical box enthusiasts are queuing up for Keith Harding's work. He has a two-year waiting list, largely for repairs for private collectors. He also services antique musical boxes that are sold by a Piccadilly store.

French Horn Maker

The French horn is so called because it was adapted from the French *cor de chasse*. The English follower of hounds is content with a simple bugle, but the French huntsman to this day can blow a magnificent tune on a multi-looped horn which he carries round his shoulder. The orchestral horn has adaptations that make it a far more sophisticated instrument. A system of valves enables the player to shorten the length of the brass tube, thereby changing the key, simply by depressing his fingers. The task of the French horn maker, as of any other musical instrument-maker, is precision. The total length of the curved tube of the horn has to be twelve feet to the nearest quarter of an inch. The valves have to be made so accurately that they are loose enough to be operated by the fingers, but not so loose that they allow the air to escape.

French horn-making in this country is synonymous with the firm of Robert Paxman of Covent Garden. Their French horns are represented in almost every major orchestra in the world. The Paxmans began in a basement in Gerrard Street towards the end of the last war and started producing instruments at the rate of two a year. They are up to 150 a year now. This is the work of some twenty men, ten of them in the London workshop and ten in another works down in Kent. 'When we started, one person was doing all the operations on one instrument. But now we've got a division of labour so that each man specializes in a particular branch of the trade; there are three branches—bell-making, valve-making and assembly.'

The bell of a horn is made on a lathe, the metal being raised on a mandrel [a tapering core of metal] made by Robert Paxman himself. 'In the hands of somebody who does not understand the subtleties of these things, you can get it very slightly wrong. But when you're in charge of the whole process yourself, then you can control every stage of it and get it absolutely right.'

The tapered tubing of the horn is made from a strip of metal cut against a template. The strip is formed into a spiral and the edges soldered together to make a tube. The joint is beaten out to an even thickness with a hammer. The tubing now has to be bent to form the loops of the horn. The craftsman fills the tube with a mixture of molten pitch and resin; when this cools it solidifies and provides a core around which the metal can be bent without distortion.

'The temperature of the pitch filling has to be correct to the nearest half-degree Centigrade. In the summer months you have got to bend it before 8.30 a.m. If it is too hot, then the pitch is too liquid and the metal buckles; if it is too cold, the pitch can snap.'

Getting together with musicians who play his instruments, Robert Paxman has managed to improve the design of the instrument to give better musical results. 'There used to be various defects built into the instrument—certain notes on the older French horns are always slightly out. In 1957 a horn player called Richard Merewether came over from Australia and introduced himself to us. He had all sorts of new ideas for the design of the instrument. He helped us to improve manufacturing methods as well as the acoustical qualities of the horn. It has become a much more efficient instrument—it now covers the whole range of notes accurately.'

Nearly all Robert Paxman's craftsmen are young, and all trained by him: 'We found that the only way to get people was to take on youngsters. We used to have an apprenticeship scheme, but we had to abandon all that nonsense—now we take on trainees. We try to retain all the people we have trained—when you have gone through all the trials and tribulations you wouldn't want them to leave and go elsewhere. It all boils down to general working conditions and remuneration.'

Robert Paxman's policy of selecting those with a deep interest in music may have something to do with his high success rate with his trainees. Out of the ten craftsmen in the London workshop there is only one who does not play some instrument or another.

Flutemaker

The three craftsmen at the Flutemakers' Guild workshops in Hackney make twelve flutes a year between them. Made to last for several lifetimes, their flutes are built in sterling silver. The cheapest costs £500 and there is a three-year waiting list for them.

The flute evolved from the simplest kind of musical instrument, a wooden tube with holes. It was developed in its present form by the German maker, Theobald Bohm, in the mid-nineteenth century. The sophisticated modern flute dates from this time; it consists essentially of a hollow tube interrupted with holes that are operated by an elaborate system of keys.

In building the keys and shaping them to fit the fingers of the player, the craftsman makes about two hundred soldered joints. This is an intricate form of silversmithing. Most of the parts for the flute are cast roughly in silver by an outside firm and the flutemaker's task is to shape each part and file it down to the correct size. Everything has to be accurate to a fraction of a millimetre. Four sizes of instrument are made—piccolos, flutes, alto flutes, and bass flutes. The bass flute is a huge instrument, four feet long, with a kink in it. The body of the piccolo is made of wood, traditionally cocus, but African blackwood is used as a substitute; it is turned and bored on the lathe.

Mr Seeley, a flutemaker who was originally trained to make bagpipes, talks about special orders:

'We have made a couple of gold instruments—some say that there's a musical difference, but it is hard for a musician to explain what the difference is. I think the gold has a heavier sound, you could put it at that. Somebody once made a left-handed flute; not only did every part have to be arranged back to front, but it was a mirror image as well. It would have been much easier for the player to learn to play it the right way round.

Recently two young men wrote out of the blue, asking to learn the trade, and we took them on as trainees. The young man comes in and says he wants to learn.

You agree to teach him. You can't say hard and fast that the chap's got to stay. We just teach them and hope they'll stay and bring back some of the money that they cost.

The old apprenticeship system was a waste of time in my opinion. You spent the first year making tea. The original idea was that you paid to learn, but in practice the apprentice was used as a form of cheap labour.'

With the two trainees, Mr Seeley hopes to build up his output of flutes to something around twenty a year. The production of London handmade flutes provides an interesting contrast with the firms that make them by machine. One American firm turns out a thousand a week.

Bell Founder

There has been a bell foundry in Whitechapel since 1570 and it has been on the present site since 1738. Fundamentally the technique of casting bells has not changed since the beginning. The same principles underlie the casting of any metal into a required shape. First a mould has to be prepared which contains a hollow of precisely the shape of the object required. Molten metal is poured into this hollow, the metal allowed to cool, and the mould removed.

It takes several weeks to prepare the moulds for a peal of bells. Each mould is made in two parts—the core and the cope. The core, which will form the inside of the mould, is built up by hand with loam, consisting largely of clay, on a foundation of bricks. The crucial point is that the outer contour of the core is going to shape the inner contour of the final bell, so the surface of the core has to be perfectly even and absolutely smooth. A form of template, known as a moulding-board, is used to make sure that the core has the same contour all round. This swivels around the central shaft on which the core is built and loam is added and smoothed down by hand until there are no gaps between the core and the moulding-board.

The cope is made on the same principle, but as it is a hollow and not a solid shape, the cope is built inside a cast-iron case. The core and the cope are dried out in the ovens and their surfaces coated with graphite to give a smooth finish. If any inscription or decoration is needed on the bell, the letters are embossed into the cope mould. Now the core is lifted onto the cope, the two are clamped together and the mould is complete.

There is something of a carnival atmosphere at the Whitechapel Bell Foundry on casting-day. There is a special excitement and magic about the casting of a peal of bells after several weeks of preparation of the moulds. A coachload of parishioners from the village that commissioned the bells may be invited to watch the process from a safe distance. The first few hours of casting-day are marked by the roar of the furnace in which the bell metal, an alloy of tin and copper, is melted. When the temperature is right, the furnace is tapped, and the glowing metal collected in a huge metal ladle suspended from a rail by a system of chains and pulleys. The surface of the molten metal is skimmed to remove impurities and the ladle is manipulated gingerly towards the row of bell moulds.

Before casting the foreman takes his cap off and beats it against the side of the ladle as if knocking off dust. It is a unconscious gesture but he does it every time and it has been built up into a kind of superstition with the other men. When the men have manipulated the ladle up to one of the moulds, at a signal from the foreman the procession stops. Very, very carefully the ladle is tipped, the foreman controlling the operation with a wheel at the side of the ladle, while a man at his side handles the chains that control the pulleys. A third man uses a scoop to guide the liquid metal into the entrance box at the head of the bell mould. The heavy metal patters into the mould, raising clouds of smoke. One after the other the moulds are filled and within twenty minutes the casting is complete.

The bells are left to cool in their moulds for two or three days. Then the copes are lifted off, the bells cleaned of any loam that adheres to their surface, and they are ready for turning. The bell is cast as nearly as possible to the required note but there is always a slight margin of error and the final tuning is done by removing metal on a lathe. On a bell-tuning lathe the bell is held vertically, upside down, and revolved against a stationary cutting blade. The tuning of the bell is tested electronically.

At Whitechapel a separate group of craftsmen is involved with the making and tuning of handbells. These are cast in sand moulds and tuned on a lathe. In tuning a handbell there is such a small margin of error that even the final polishing of a bell makes a difference to its tone. There are 61 bells in a set of handbells and they are tuned together and tested electronically as one instrument.

For the bicentennial celebration of American Independence in 1976, the foundry cast a number of replicas of the Liberty bell. They were well qualified to do this, since it was at Whitechapel that the original was cast. Cast here too were the bells for Westminster Abbey. Two of these were cast in 1583 and 1598 by Robert Mot, the first bellfounder at Whitechapel. His successors have cast, or recast, the remainder, so that the complete peal of bells at Westminster spans some 350 years.

Also among the many famous bells cast here are Big Ben, Bow bells and the bells of St Clement Danes in the Strand, which play the tune, 'Oranges and Lemons' at certain hours of the day.

PART VI

Books and printing

This is an area of the crafts that is perhaps, most closely related to art. The work of many craftsmen in this group are vehicles for another person's art. In such cases the best craftsmanship is invisible, and the best craftsmen anonymous, suppressing their own individuality.

Vellum Maker

Although the Chinese have been making paper for something like 2,500 years it was not introduced into England until the fifteenth century. Before that time the scribes and illuminators used vellum and parchment for their work. They still do. Vellum and parchment provide a smooth and supple surface for fine work, and they are stronger and more durable than paper. Vellum is made from the hides of calves and goats and it is suitable for drums and bookbindings as well as for writing and illumination. Parchment is much finer and is made from the inner lining of the skin of the sheep.

London was traditionally one of the centres of the vellum trade and even after the war there were several firms, mostly south of the Thames, making vellum. But only one firm has survived—H. Band and Co. And within this firm only one man is employed full-time at this ancient craft—Jim Ellender.

The animal skins come in with a certain amount of hair and fat attached. They have to be soaked in lime for some weeks and the hair and fat are stripped off mechanically before they are ready for the craftsman. He takes a skin from the bath in which it is soaking and ties it onto a wooden frame. The hide is stretched until it is taut and absolutely flat, and now the delicate operation begins. The hide has to be shaved so that the outer layer is stripped off, leaving a surface that is absolutely smooth and free from bumps. The vellum-maker uses a knife with a semi-circular blade and the handle set at right-angles to it. He shaves the hide with a sweeping motion of the blade. The skill lies in putting just the right amount of pressure on the knife so that it shaves evenly, but does not cut a hole through the hide.

Every job is ordered or 'bespoken' by the customer, and different amounts are shaved off by the craftsman according to the thickness of the vellum required. Also every hide is different from the next one. Jim Ellender explains:

'Every skin has got its own personality. Each one has a different weight. One skin takes a long time; the next one might be quite different and take half the time. Norwegian skins are very fine. English skins are a little coarser; I think it depends on the climate and what the animals eat.

You know the old plastic has knocked the stuffing out of this job. We used to do vellum for all the drum-makers in the country. We used to do drum jobs for the Army and the Navy, but now it's all plastic—unless they want something for a really big drum, and then we usually do it.

I have been working here for twenty-five years. Apart from us there's one other firm in the country and that's it. One woman, she's a scribe, she comes in to order her vellum and she says to me, "Don't pack it up, it's my living." She's just one of hundreds who depend on us.

It's a shame these jobs are going the way they are these days. It's hard work, mind, shaving hides all day. But it's got its compensations, you know. You get satisfaction from it and you can't say that of many jobs these days.'

If the vellum-makers disappear altogether it would be a fatal blow for the scribes and illuminators. This is just another example of how closely the different trades depend on each other for their survival.

Bookbinder

The book that you are reading has been bound entirely by machine, and no craftsman has had a hand in it. The mass of modern books are bound in this way and this has been the case since the middle of the last century. Before that time books were hand-bound of necessity. Now hand-binding is a luxury and is carried out by three more or less distinct groups of craftsmen.

The first group are the individualists, the creative bookbinders, the finest of whom are members of a society called 'Designer Bookbinders'. Some of them are amateurs in the sense that they do not make a living at their craft, and most of them work from home, carrying out the forty or more separate bookbinding processes single-handed. Most of their work is commissioned by collectors. In this group the emphasis is on fine design and inventive techniques, and the designer bookbinders can be regarded as artists who choose to express themselves in the medium of bookbinding.

The second group deals with the restoration and replacement of old bindings. The British Library has the largest bindery of this sort, and the craftsmen there, like the painters of the Forth Bridge, are permanently involved with the continuous cycle of restoration and decay.

The third group are the trade binderies, the commercial craftsmen who carry on the traditional styles and techniques of hand bookbinding for lectern Bibles, commemorative volumes and the like. Usually there is a division of labour in the trade binderies, with craftsmen specializing in different stages of the process. The trade binders learn their skills by apprenticeship and their professional conduct is controlled by a union.

One of the longest-established trade firms in London is W. T. Morrell, founded in Soho in 1860. They have been in their present premises in Covent Garden for over sixty years. Here the craftsmen still use the boxwood presses, the mahogany sewing frames and the brass tools that have been used every day since the firm began. The workshop is mellow with the rich colours of the leather-bound books

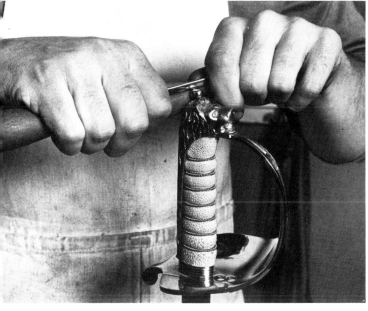

Jim Ellender is the only vellum maker in the London area. Here he shaves down a stretched calf hide, which is destined, as vellum, to be used for a drum, a bookbinding or as a surface for a legal document or an illuminated inscription.

The handle of a naval sword is covered with the skin of a Pacific shark. This is stretched, when damp, over a carved wooden base. Here a craftsman in Joseph Starkey's Walworth workshop burnishes the gold embellishments on a handle.

Hatmakers' equipment. Left, boxwood blocks for top hats. There is a different block for each size of hat and each block is made in five parts. This makes it possible to get the block out after a hat has hardened around it.

The conformateur, a cunning device to record the shape of a customer's head. The white card is a record of a particular customer's fitting. When the card is fitted into this machine the wooden bars around the circumference reproduce the conformation of the customer's head. The hatmaker follows this guide when shaping the hat.

Bert Bonnell is hat shaper for Sam Patey's firm off the Walworth Road. His job is to coax the pliant brim of a top hat into an elegant curve and to fit the hat to a particular customer's head. In the weeks leading up to Ascot he has several thousand toppers to repair.

The boot-tree maker's workbench at Lobb's shop in St James's. Tom van Steenhoven uses the traditional bench knife to carve an accurate wooden replica of each particular foot. Each bump and depression is faithfully reproduced on the last on which the shoe is built, and again on the tree which is made to keep the shoe in shape.

Architectural sculpture at St Paul's Cathedral. Kenneth Gardner carves directly into the stone without making preliminary drawings. This urn will replace the original by Caius Cibber outside St Paul's. Kenneth Gardner grew up in this trade – his father and grandfather were architectural sculptors before him.

and the patina of the wooden fittings. The craftsmen work in silence, giving the place the monastic atmosphere of an ancient scholars' library.

The preliminary sewing of the folded paper sections of a book is traditionally women's work, and at Morrell's it is carried out by a lady who comes part-time. She sews the sections onto strong vertical bands which are held vertically in the sewing-frame.

Next, the sections pass to the 'forwarder' who is the craftsman who deals with foundations of the binding. He sews on the boards, trims the pages with a sharp-bladed tool, the plough, and makes ready the binding for the finishers. The forwarder's work is hidden in the final binding, but it provides the basis of it. As Morrell's forwarder colourfully puts it: 'It's like a woman: You can put loads of make-up on, but if the foundation isn't any good she looks ugly all the same.'

The finisher has the most prestigious job and enjoys the highest rate of pay. He puts the outer covering of leather on the binding, and adds the lettering and the decorative patterns which are impressed into the leather with heated tools. 'Blind tooling' is the straightforward impression of the hot tools in the leather. In 'gold tooling', the craftsman fills the impressions with genuine gold leaf. This is done by brushing white of egg, known as 'glair', onto the leather, laying gold leaf over it, and then pressing into the gold with the heated tool. The heat causes the glair to coagulate and the gold sticks to the leather. The excess gold can then be brushed away.

Mr Davies is the chief finisher at Morrell's and he has been with the firm since before the war:

> 'It's always been my policy to keep the standards up. There's a lot of bad work around. I call it a kind of deceit. They use the best materials but they don't sew the books together properly and they fall to bits.
>
> You can't be an apprentice over twenty-one. So the later the school-leaving age, the shorter the apprenticeship becomes. It's now about five years. So much depends on the individual. If he grasps it he just gets ahead. Gradually he gets better each week and each month. It never used to be like that, you know. They used to hold the apprentices back. In the slump period they were frightened that the young people would put them out of work. I've known people before the war to gild a book and then strip it all off again. Then they'd do the whole thing again, just to create more work. It came to such a pass that some men were told to go home and the firms said that they would let them know if there was any more work. That's when a lot of craftsmen left the trade. Now there's plenty of work, but we can't get the men.'

There used to be twelve craftsmen working at the benches in Morrell's finishing room. Now there are only three. The skilled bookbinder is very much in demand now, and the future is rosy; but the depression in the trade before the war meant a break in continuity which is still proving very difficult to heal.

Edge-gilder

The edge-gilder lays down a fine layer of gold leaf onto the edges of pages of fine books such as Bibles and commemorative volumes. Playing-cards and invitations are often gilded too.

The gilding of a book is done half-way through the bookbinding process, after the pages have been sewn together but before the covers are added. Several books of the same size may be gilded at once. The gilder lines up the books, edges uppermost, in a boxwood press like a huge carpenter's vice. When the press is screwed tight the books are forced together with a pressure of up to five tons. Now there are no gaps between the pages and the edges of the books form a continuous flat surface to be gilded.

French chalk is dusted onto the surface to prevent liquid penetrating the pages. Next, as a foundation for the gold, a coat of starch solution is brushed on, followed by a layer of gelatine. Now comes the most skilled part of the process, the laying of the gold leaf. Gold leaf is so light that the slightest puff of air will shift it. To pick up gold leaf, the gilder rubs a piece of card lightly against his hair: this creates enough static electricity for the leaf to be picked up by the card and to cling to it. With a puff of breath and a gentle stroking motion of the card, he lifts the gold off the card and onto the book. He has to get the gold to land flat and also place it accurately to prevent wastage.

Now the gilder rubs the gold surface with a 'burnisher', a tool consisting of a highly polished stone set into a wooden handle. By burnishing the gold he presses it into the gelatine base where it remains permanently fixed. When the books are taken out of the press, one flick through is enough to split the gold and separate the pages.

When cards are to be gilded they are held at a slant in a much smaller press, then scraped with a blade to make a bevelled edge onto which the gold leaf is laid down.

G. H. Patmore gilds cards for the stationery trade and also gilds a few books for private customers. He is past retiring age, but works at a tremendous speed and never pauses for a rest:

'Many years ago everyone in the trade used to do piecework. The more you did, the more you got paid. So I got used to working fast. Now I can't slow down. It's not a question of the money. I could earn enough in three days to suit my needs. It might sound silly to some people, but I like work. I get here at 7.0 and I knock off at 5.0. I work Saturday mornings until 12.30 because I find it easier than staying at home doing the shopping.

My father was in this trade and so was my grandfather. My son works with me. My son and me, we'll be the last. I came up to retiring age last year, but I won't retire. I know that when I can't push my bike any more it'll be time for me to pack up.

I've been doing it for forty-eight years, so no wonder it looks easy. Look at this batch of cards; it looks a lot, but it only fetches me thirty bob when I've finished. If I'm in a good mood I can do five thousand cards in a day.

There are no apprentices now. The unions put a stop to that, you know. They said there had to be six people working in a firm before it was permitted to take on an apprentice. Well, there are not many gilders that employ that number of men. The way I look at it, the bigger you are, the bigger your headaches.

I'm a card gilder myself. I've gilded half a million playing cards for Waddingtons, and I used to do work for Letts the diary people. When I set out on my own I reckoned that it was no good saying no to work. So I accept book-work too. I thought that if I could do the small diaries for Letts then I could do the bigger books as well. I'm a great believer that if there's a man can do something, then I can. Because that man's made just the same as me. If a man's got a skill, it just means he's using his brain better. If you set your mind to it, you know, you can do anything.'

Several gilding firms have closed down in London recently. Eventually bookbinders who want the extra refinement of gilded edges on their books will have to do it themselves. When one trade declines, the others have to become less specialized and each craftsman a jack of all trades.

Copperplate Engraver

In the eighteenth and early nineteenth centuries the designs for trade-cards, songsheets and the like were engraved on flat 'plates' of copper and printed from them. The copperplate engravers used a flowing style and embellished their lettering with elegant swirls and flourishes. Their technique gave its name to their style and their brand of lettering became known as 'copperplate'. For a time, copperplate handwriting was taught in schools, but now the style has declined and survives only among the few remaining copperplate engravers themselves who still use it for wedding invitations, letterheads and visiting cards.

A well-engraved wedding invitation in the traditional copperplate style is one of the loveliest examples of commercial printing that can still be obtained today. The letters have been fashioned and spaced by hand and eye, and the subtle changes in thickness of the lines are achieved by slight changes in pressure of the craftsman's hand. When printed, the letters stand out from the paper as if embossed.

The copperplate engraver cuts grooves into the smooth surface of a copper plate with a sharply pointed tool with a tapering tip, known as a burin. He guides the line by moving the plate itself on a rounded pad of leather, while pushing the burin forward. He skirts lightly over the surface for a fine shallow line and digs deeper to thicken the line. If he makes a mistake he is faced with the laborious task of scraping away at the copper to remove the engraved line, hammering the plate flat from the back, and smoothing the surface down with a burnisher.

Stan Apsey, who works in a small room in a quiet side street in Clerkenwell, learnt the trade from his father. He has a cheerfully disgruntled attitude to his trade:

'I charge about 50p for ten letters. I can make £20 in a good day, working hard. But when I haven't got work I grouse. I've had two really bad months now. I have enough work to see me through today and that's it. This trade is like a barometer, you see; it's the first to go when there's any kind of economic trouble.

It's all very well making things, but it's no bloody use if nobody can afford to buy them. Nobody wants a craftsman these days in a capitalist society. What with the self-employed stamp, the rates and travelling costs, the overheads are enormous. And in this trade the end-product is too small to make it pay. The difference between a profit and a loss might only be a matter of pence. Mind you, the trade has been dying for two or three hundred years and it hasn't gone yet. It was already dying when I started learning from my Dad.

I used to have a mate here who did all my printing for me. But he has a job in a theatre down the West End now. He does the cleaning up after the shows. When he works overtime and does the stage door as well he earns up to £135 a week. Mind you, that's working about 24 hours a day. But he loves it. Never been so happy in his life.

If you ask me, engraving is only good for the halt, the blind and the daft. I'm thinking of giving it up and getting a job.'

There is a cheap form of copperplate printing, with the letters typeset and printed by letterpress and lithography. But it has a uniform and impersonal appearance that is an insult to the engraver's art.

Copperplate Printer

The engravings that were used to illustrate eighteenth and nineteenth-century books were printed individually by hand. The craft of engraving as a technique of reproduction disappeared just as soon as photographic reproduction made it dispensable. Nevertheless, fine printing lived on, and there is a firm of printers in Putney who flourish now, as they have flourished for almost 150 years on the business of printing engraved copper plates. In the nineteenth century, Thomas Ross was one of the leading London printers of book plates, visiting cards and engraved reproductions of paintings; they thrive now on reprinting from their enormous stock of eighteenth and nineteenth-century engraved copper plates. These are now faced with steel, to protect them from wear.

Huge sporting and military prints, rural landscapes and reproductions of paintings by popular English masters like Romney and Landseer, are printed from the original plates on massive hand-presses, weighing up to two tons, that have been in constant use for a century. Simply by continuing to do the work that they have done for so long, this ancient firm is effectively producing 'antiques'—and there is a roaring trade for their prints in America and Italy. But Ross's are careful not to deceive collectors and, by using modern papers, they make it clear that their prints are recent impressions from old plates.

The young printers are taken on straight from school and learn the trade at Ross's under the master printer, Philip McQueen. Himself a veteran of the trade since 1918, Mr McQueen is the fifth generation of a family who have been printers since before 1800.

Briefly, the principles of copperplate printing are these: the first and most delicate stage of the process is the inking of the plate. The grooves and recesses engraved in the plate have to be filled with ink. This is straightforward enough if the whole plate is to be printed in black, but for a coloured print, each area of colour has to be inked separately by hand, the ink being smeared on with a rag or a finger, or painted into the grooves with a brush. Now the surface of the plate is wiped clean with rags so that the ink rests only in the grooves. By leaving varying amounts of ink on the surface the printer can control the tone and brightness of different areas of the print. Dry chalk is used to clean all traces of ink from the edges and margins of the plate.

The plate is then warmed, to make the ink more fluid for printing, and laid on the flat bed of the press. Heavy hand-made paper, lightly damped, is laid down over the plate, and three soft felts, known as blankets, are put down on top of that. By winding the geared wheel of the press, the printer pulls the plate, paper and blankets between two heavy rollers, under great pressure. The pressure forces the paper into the grooves on the plate, where it picks up all the ink. To some extent the paper itself retains the shape of the grooves, which accounts for the beautiful surface relief which is characteristic of this printing method and none other.

Printing in one colour, the craftsmen at Ross's can produce 25 to 40 impressions in a day, depending on the size and complexity of a plate. But if several colours are needed the inking of the plate is such a lengthy operation that only one or two impressions can be produced in a day. To save time and expense, colour prints are mostly made these days by printing in black and colouring by hand with watercolour afterwards. For this work Ross's employ a full-time craftsman. This is a complex skill in itself, even the simplest sky requiring washes of five different colours.

With printed engravings it was customary for the artist who designed the plate, and the craftsmen who engraved it, to have their names included just below the printed image. The printer was usually anonymous, in spite of the fact that his craftsmanship made a rich contribution to the final product.

Music Engraver

The clearest and most legible, as well as the most attractive, sheet music is reproduced from hand-engraved plates. Here is a unique trade, quite distinct from the engraving of printed words and illustrations. In contrast to the copperplate engraver, the music engraver works on soft pewter plates. He forms the notes by tapping suitably shaped steel punches into the plate with a hammer; he completes the notes by engraving tails and cross-bars by hand. And, unlike copperplate printing, the music is not printed directly from the engraved plates. Only a few proofs are printed from each, and these form the basis for reproduction by another method, such as lithography.

There are a few music engravers on the Continent and a handful in this country, including just one man in London, and that is the full surviving complement of a trade that once kept thousands of craftsmen in work.

London's lone music engraver is Fred Chapman of the Curwen Press at Plaistow. Now in his seventies, Fred Chapman completed his six-year apprenticeship almost half a century ago. In the years that he has practised his trade he has developed such facility with his tools, such sensitivity of eye, that he seems to place each note instinctively in the correct position on the page, in perfect visual harmony with its neighbours. His pages of music look inevitable; the craftsmanship is quite unobtrusive. The engraved page is simply a vehicle for the music. Here, as in so many of the hand trades, the best craftsmanship is invisible, and not usually noticed until it disappears.

Unusually for an engraver, Fred Chapman can read the music that he engraves. If anything this is a slight disadvantage because the engraver works from right to left on a page, against the direction of the music. First he measures out the plate and marks the points where the staves (five parallel lines) will go. Then he cuts the staves into the plate with a five-pronged tool, held against a straight edge. With his dividers he marks out the spaces between the notes—this process, known as 'writing up', is probably the most skilled in the whole operation; every note must be placed so that the page is well balanced, while faithfully following the score.

Now he is ready to use his punches. He starts by putting in any text that is to accompany the music, punching each letter individually into the plate. The notes are left until last. For the head of each note the punch is hammered into the plate with some force, making bumps at the back of the plate which have to be hammered flat again later. Next the tails and crossbars of the notes are engraved by hand—this is the most personal part of the work and every engraver has his own recognizable style.

Finally the plate is cleaned up, and the first proof taken from it. This proof is sent to the composer for correction—a time of dread for the engraver, because corrections are frantically difficult to make. If the composer changes his mind about anything, each faulty note has to be smoothed out by hammering through from the back of the plate. Most alterations upset the visual balance of the plate so much that the engraver has to start all over again.

Music engraving is slow and laborious work and it costs a publisher so much to have each page engraved that he has to sell thousands of copies of a work to cover his costs; and only the great classics sell that number. The sad truth is that there are other cheaper, if less elegant ways of printing music (the music typewriter is one of them) and the craft of the music engraver is unlikely to survive much longer.

Wood Engravers' Blockmaker

Wood-engraving is a form of printmaking in which the artist cuts his designs into the surface of a flat block of boxwood and prints from the surface of the wood. The engraved design appears as white against black in the finished print. The greatest wood engraver of all time was Thomas Bewick, the eighteenth-century Newcastle engraver who invented the technique of engraving on the endgrain of boxwood. Boxwood has such a close grain that it is possible to engrave extremely fine details into it.

Since Bewick's time, the standard of English wood engraving has been very high, and one of the reasons is that since 1859 the English artists have been fortunate with their blockmakers. In that year the firm of T. N. Lawrence and Son was established. The first Mr Lawrence supplied the commercial artists who engraved the illustrations for the popular books and magazines of the time. The present Mr

Lawrence, grandson of the founder, is a famous character in the art world and has made blocks for some of the most distinguished artists since the 1920s.

'The craft of wood engraving has been on the decline, but it is coming up a bit again now. We do a lot of blocks for the art schools and there are a few young engravers producing lovely work. But you should see the coarse rubbish that some of them turn out these days. I tell them that they could do it just as well on lino.'

Mr Lawrence is understandably upset to see engravers doing crude work on his exquisitely made blocks. Each block is made from several small pieces of boxwood glued together; the box tree is extremely slow-growing and it is rare to find a piece more than a few inches wide. Each piece is hand-planed so that the edges are perfectly flat and smooth. The pieces are jointed and glued together with hot gelatine glue which is put on extremely thinly so that there is not the slightest gap between the wood sections. The whole block is planed and finished by hand to make a glass-smooth surface for engraving. The test of the craftsman's skill is to get the surface perfectly flat so that the block prints evenly.

Silkscreen Printmaker

In Paris there has been a long tradition of studio printmaking in which very fine craftsmen printers produce etchings and lithographs for painters and sculptors. The relationship between artist and craftsman is a creative one, and the craftsman's skill can stimulate an artist to do work that he might not otherwise have thought possible. Working at the *ateliers* of the craftsmen printers, artists such as Toulouse-Lautrec, Bonnard, Picasso and Braque did some of their finest work in the medium of printmaking.

In England the tradition has not been so strong, but in the early 1960s there emerged in London a printmaking studio which changed the picture almost overnight. The studio is called Kelpra. It was started by Christopher Prater, and the printing technique is silkscreen.

Silkscreen is a relatively young technique, evolving in the nineteenth century from stencil-printing. Originally used for printing wallpapers and flags, it was a technique little used by artists for fine prints—until Christopher Prater started Kelpra studio. Silkscreen lends itself to images that demand areas of flat, opaque colour, and it is not so well suited as etching and lithography to subtle hand-drawn images. But in the early 1960s the time was ripe for silkscreen to come into its own. Pop art and hard-edge abstraction were the liveliest art movements of the time and both styles demanded flat areas of bright colour. And Christopher Prater, who was printing posters for the Arts Council and the Royal Academy at the time, was using silkscreen in a more subtle and sensitive way than it had been used before. He made a print for the artist Richard Hamilton, and another for Eduardo Paolozzi. The word spread, and since then Prater has made prints for almost every British artist of distinction of that generation. In fifteen years he has produced 2,500 artists' prints and an example of every one of them is now deposited with the Tate Gallery—a unique honour for a printmaker.

The principle of silkscreen printing is very simple. The screen is made of a very fine-meshed silk, stretched over a frame. The frame is hinged to the bench so that it can be lifted and the printing paper slipped under it. Each colour is printed separately. A gob of coloured ink is laid on top of the screen, and is then pulled across it with a flat rubber tool called a 'squeegee'. This pushes the ink through the tiny pores of the screen on to the paper below. To obtain the image that the artist wants, areas of the screen are masked off with a solution that blocks the pores between the silk so that the ink cannot get through. This mask can be drawn onto the screen by hand, or it can be made photographically from a drawn or photographic image supplied by the artist.

At Kelpra the photographic preparation of the image on the screen and its actual printing is fairly mechanical, though carried out with unusual care. Christopher Prater's special contribution to the trade is his attention to every detail. Contrary to commercial practice, he does not take time into account. Some prints are developed and improved over a period of years. Prater immerses himself in the work of every artist that he deals with. 'You have to subdue personal preferences, and become a kind of chameleon.'

One of Prater's most creative partnerships is with the painter R. B. Kitaj. Kitaj works from a host of printed and drawn images, collected over the years, each one patiently photographed by Prater to make a kind of memory bank for the artist to draw upon at any time. When Kitaj has an idea for a print, Prater might receive instructions from the artist in the form of a tiny sketch on a scrap of paper, with brief notes about the colours and size of the print and the type of paper to be used. Prater is so familiar with the artist's thought-processes that these shorthand notes are quite enough for him to make the first proofs of the print. This serves as a working drawing on which the artist builds up more and more images until the print is complete. Kitaj's prints develop slowly in this way, over a long period. On one of the final prints there were 81 colours, each of which had to be printed separately by hand.

Prater's most fruitful working relationships have been with artists around his own age: 'With the middle generation artists there was always that link with the pioneering days. With those first Richard Hamilton prints in the early 1960s we used to sell the first twenty for £4 each to pay for the printing. But the younger generation don't know about this, and we've become part of the establishment to them.'

Unfortunately there seem to be very few young artists at the moment who can think at secondhand, and direct their work through a craftsman printer, even one as sensitive and adaptable as Christopher Prater.

PART VII

Clothes and sundries

Hand craftsmanship in this field has survived, in most cases, not because it is the only way to make a thing, but the best way. The luxury of handmade clothes is the prerogative of the rich. The relationship between craftsman and patron is such that when the prevailing economic policy is to squeeze the rich, some of the first people to feel the effect are the tailors of Soho and the top-hat makers south of the Thames.

Top-hat Maker

Top hats, academic mortar-boards, riding hats; hats for Beefeaters, Chelsea Pensioners and hotel doormen—all kinds of hard hats are made by the firm of S. Patey in Walworth, South London. All hats are made to measure and all processes are carried out by hand. Patey's is the last surviving firm making top hats in England. Just after the last war there were fourteen firms in London and several in the provinces, but since then the fashion for formal dress has declined and one by one the top-hat makers have gone out of business.

Mr Patey's workshop is a far cry from the elegant showrooms of the West End hatters where most of his hats are ordered. The steam and heat from the hot irons gives the place something of the atmosphere of a Victorian sweat-shop. A line of young men, bare to the waist, wield hot irons at one end of the room. At the other end, a row of women at a table are hectically stitching the covers and linings of the hats. Between the two groups are three specialist craftsmen who make the top hats. The 'bodymaker' builds the foundation of the hat; the 'finisher' covers it with material; the 'shaper' moulds the brim of the hat into its characteristic curved form and shapes the rim of the hat to fit a particular customer's head.

The substance secreted by an insect to make its protective cocoon is the basis for the hard hat that protects a man's head when he falls from his horse. The substance is shellac, and it is imported by Patey's at a huge price from India. The body of a hat is made from stretched cotton dipped into melted shellac and then dried. The shellac-impregnated cotton, known as 'gossamer' in the trade, is a stiff material of great strength. It is ideal for making hats because it can be pressed and moulded into any shape with a hot iron, and it keeps its shape when it cools. Also the hot iron melts the shellac which then acts as a glue, and will hold any material that is pressed on to it.

The craftsman known as the 'bodymaker' builds the crown of a top hat by ironing several layers of gossamer around a wooden hat block of the required shape and size. An ordinary topper is made from four layers of gossamer: a hunting topper has two more layers for extra strength. Every size of hat requires a different-sized block. For the brim of the hat the layers of gossamer are first ironed flat and then shaped with the iron on a slightly arched wooden mould. A hole is cut for the crown and then the brim and the crown are sealed together with the iron. Now the hat is ready for covering.

The very best top hats used to be covered with a black cloth made with tufts of the finest silk. But the supplies of this material are rapidly running out and soon all black toppers will be covered with a velour substitute. The cloth is cut to size and stitched by the seamstresses; this is a precision job as one of the seams runs along the top edge of the hat and has to be perfectly accurate. The finisher's work involves the delicate operation of ironing the covering material on to the body of the hat so that it lies perfectly flat without a wrinkle anywhere. The material is put on wet, and as he works the finisher constantly brushes the material so that the fibres all point the same way around the sides of the hat; he spins the hat under the brush to create the corkscrew twirl of silk on the top. After the finisher has done his part the hat is still far from finished. The linings have to be stitched, and then the hat is ready for shaping.

To shape the tilt and curl of the brim of a top hat the shaper softens the hat with heat from an iron and then moulds the brim around a number of handmade tools of wood and brass. The shaping of the hat is the most skilled branch of the trade; a certain amount can be achieved by measurement, but the final stylish tilt of the brim can only be judged by eye.

Harry Parbott has been in the trade as a finisher for thirty-five years:

'I believe I'm the last person in the trade to have done the apprenticeship. I signed on for seven years in 1935. First they used to have you out doing the deliveries; then they put you on the bench for a month to see if you liked the trade. The next thing, they got on to the union. It was still going then, the Hatters' Union, but it folded up in 1942. Next thing, your parents were approached—were they willing to have you indentured? If they were willing, the chap who was going to teach you, he had to consent. Then they got the indenture papers and all the people had to sign; yourself, the secretary of the union, the shop steward, the governor, your father, the master craftsman—they all had to sign the papers. It was a tradition and it was something that had been tried and proved. You see in 1935 there were two million unemployed, and I was being offered a secure job for seven years; that was something, you know. When I started I got 12/- a week for a five-day week. But as an apprentice you had to pay back a third of your wage to the employer for teaching you.

Then in 1939 I went to the war. When I came back I still had two years of my apprenticeship to run. But they waived it. I didn't realize it at the time, but the indenture scheme was finished. The war changed everything.

This trade has given me a lot of interest over the years. I wouldn't say that it's given me a good living; only a fair one. I sometimes think I could have done better.'

Hatmakers have been called 'gentlemen journeymen hatters' ever since Elizabeth I, on a journey to Tilbury, asked who a group of smartly dressed citizens in beaver hats might be. When told that they were the journeymen hatters of Southwark, she replied 'Then such journeymen must be gentlemen'. And the hatters have worn that hat ever since.

Bespoke Tailor and Cutter

The great tailoring businesses of Savile Row have imposing façades and grand interiors that can be somewhat daunting. But the splendour of these establishments and the prestige of Savile Row itself rests upon the slightly bent shoulders of two or three hundred anonymous master tailors who work behind the scenes, either on the premises or in small independent workrooms around the West End. The quality of Savile Row work has been unequalled throughout the world for a century and still the world comes here to buy the best tailoring that is available anywhere.

Bespoke means made to measure, and if you wish to be measured for a Savile Row suit you will need to pay anything from £200 upwards. It takes two months for the work to be done, and during that time you will be asked to return at least twice for fittings. If you are in a desperate hurry the whole process can be speeded up to a little under a week. A master tailor can make up a jacket in two days and a pair of trousers in a day, and he can, if necessary, dispense with the intermediate fittings. Provided that you look after it, your Savile Row suit will last for twenty or thirty years. Even after that time it is more likely that it will be the decline of your figure and not of your suit that will force you to part company with it.

When the naval tailoring firm of Gieves merged in 1974 with the predominantly military house of Hawkes, the staff of the two firms were all accommodated in the Hawkes's workrooms at No. 1 Savile Row. The firm has a regular flow of service and livery uniform work, but men's civilian suits are the main bulk of the work. Upstairs at Gieves and Hawkes the work force is as cosmopolitan as the customers they serve. In the main workroom there are Greeks, and Chinese, Cypriots and Italians, English and Yugoslavians, Portuguese and Austrians. All of them are master tailors, but each one specializes in a particular branch of the trade. One team of tailors works on the jackets and a separate group on the trousers.

Traditionally tailors were always men, with women assistants doing the finishing jobs such as sewing on the trimmings like buttons and linings. But this distinction is being broken down and there are now several fully qualified tailoresses on the Gieves and Hawkes payroll. Nearly all the work is done on the premises, but some of the finishing is given to outworkers who visit once a week to deliver and collect their work.

The cutter is the craftsman who supervises the whole operation of making a suit. He is the man in the middle, who takes instructions from the customer and feeds work to the tailors.

A good suit is said to be 'well cut', and the success of a garment depends on the cutter's skill. From a set of measurements, usually twelve, the cutter draws up the patterns for a suit, with a sharp slither of chalk on stiff brown paper. The paper patterns are cut out, and the cutter draws around them on to the cloth. Each piece of cloth must be cut with a thought for the finished appearance of the suit. A patterned cloth must be cut so that adjacent pieces match and the stripes or checks line up across seams, darts, and pockets.

In the tailors' workroom, the garment is assembled very roughly for the first time. This is called basting and white cotton is used, in large stitches. At the first fitting the customer is in for a bit of a shock. His suit looks crude and messy, criss-crossed with lines of white cotton, and there are no pockets or lapels. But this fitting is for the cutter's benefit alone; he judges the fit and chalks onto the cloth any adjustments that need to be made. The suit is taken back to the workroom where it is taken apart, adjusted and reassembled. It is more precisely shaped and the lapels and pockets are added, so that when the customer returns for the second fitting he can judge more accurately how his finished suit will look and feel. If everything is approved, then the suit passes back to the tailors to be remade and finished. This time reinforcements are built into the shoulders, collars and sleeves—as Mr Jones, the head cutter at Gieves and Hawkes, says: 'It's the little invisible details inside a coat that hold it together, give it line, and put life into it.'

The tailor's craft is something like sculpture, in which the tailor fashions a hollow shell to fit an existing form of known shape and dimensions. He gives a flat material breadth as well as length and height. One of the tailor's highest skills is in moulding the material by damping it and shaping it with a hot iron, to follow a three-dimensional contour. Here lies the difference between a bespoke suit and a ready-made one. However well it is cut, the ready-made suit is merely stitched together to follow the contours of a generalized body. In making a bespoke suit, the tailor coaxes the cloth into shape to fit one particular body with precision. As he sews, he applies tension to the cloth here, releases it a little there, and continually moulds and shapes the cloth by damping and ironing. With his head bent to his work the master tailor loses himself in concentration, carried away by the mixture of mathematics and art that is his trade.

Mr Tassos is a Cypriot who learnt the trade in his own country but now works as foreman trouser tailor at Gieves and Hawkes. 'Some people are born to be tailors. If you have it, you can do anything, from start to finish. I wouldn't say flair, I would say it's an art. It's like riding a bicycle; once you can make a coat or suit you never forget how to do it. You don't need education for it. You don't need grammar, but you do need intelligence. Tailoring in Cyprus was for people who wanted to get on, but didn't have the means to educate themselves. I wanted to be a doctor, but I didn't have the education for it. Here I am, though, still cutting things.'

There is a friendly community atmosphere in the workrooms at Gieves and Hawkes. The comradeship between tailors must have been even stronger in the past, when tailors were more segregated from the rest of working society. Until the last war, tailors were abused by long hours, poor working conditions, meagre pay and often racial discrimination. Inevitably they took refuge in their own groups and, as any enclosed or persecuted minority does, they developed their own language and

Making French horns at
Robert Paxman's workshop in
Covent Garden. The craftsman
is preparing to hammer the
seam of a horn tube, to flatten
it; the tube is filled with pitch
so that it does not buckle
when hammered. Earmuffs
are a sensible precaution
against the sharp noise of the
hammer.

The flutemaker's workbench,
with two piccolos and a
concert flute under construction.
There are two hundred soldered
joints in a flute. The flute was
developed in its sophisticated
form in the 1840s.

Ron Mickish carving a piano bridge for a Broadwood grand. The sound-board supports his weight; it has to withstand a tension of half a ton when the piano is strung. Beethoven, Chopin and Liszt gave enthusiastic testimonials for pianos made in London by the Broadwood firm.

Tuning a bell at the Whitechapel foundry. The bell is rotated on a lathe and the bell is tuned by shaving metal from its inner surface.

ritual which is almost incomprehensible to outsiders. Every trade has its own jargon and expressions, but the tailors' is richer than most. Some of their expressions, like 'kicking your heels', have entered the language and are now in general use outside the trade.

Glossary of Tailors' Phrases

Kipper. Tailor's woman assistant. Called kippers because they always worked in pairs. This was for their own safety—a kind of chaperone system, so that the one could protect the other if the tailor made advances.

Can you spare the boot? Can you give me a loan? Dating from the time that all tailors used to sit cross-legged at the bench. The tailor would record a loan by chalking it up on the sole of his boot.

Mungo. Cloth cuttings. These belong to the tailor, and he can earn a few pennies by selling them to a rag merchant.

Bunce. A perk of the trade. So mungo is one type of tailor's bunce.

Crib. Larger scraps of cloth, saved from a length of cloth allotted for a job. The crib could be used to make a skirt or a pair of trousers. Another example of a tailor's bunce.

On the log. Piecework. As in most trades before the war, and some even now, tailors were paid according to the quantity of work they turned out. The work was logged up against the tailor's name in the book.

To have a balloon. To have no money coming in at the end of the week.

Dead. A job is dead when it's been paid for already. So there is no money coming in for it, and it is as well to get it off your hands quickly.

In the drag. Late with a job of work.

Rubbing in a PT. Fitting in a private job, e.g., making yourself a pair of trousers during the lunch break. This practice is allowed in most workrooms provided the tailors are discreet about it, and do it in their own time.

Duck shoving. An East End expression, meaning making the stitches too big. The equivalent West End expression is 'skipping it'.

Tweed merchant. A tailor who does the easy work. A term of contempt for a poor workman, because tweed being soft and rough is easier to work than other cloths.

Soft sew. A cloth that is easy to work, e.g., tweed.

A bit of old schmutter. A piece of poor cloth, rag. (A Jewish expression).

Bodger. A term used in all trades to describe a craftsman who makes a rough job.

Codger. A tailor who does up old suits.

Doctor. An alteration tailor. A separate trade in most houses.

Chancer. Someone who chances his arm, i.e., a tailor who applies for a job and says he can do anything when he cannot.

Barring. The equivalent of 'present company excepted', e.g. 'This shop is a load of bodgers, barring', means barring the person you are talking to.

Small seams. A warning expression to a fellow tailor that the person you are talking about is coming into the room.

Umsies. A name to describe someone who is in the room whom you are talking about, but you do not want him to know it. Even if he does hear, there is an element of doubt in his mind about who you are referring to.

On the cod. Gone for a drink.

Kicking. Looking for another job. If he is dissatisfied with where he is, a tailor might go out kicking during his lunch break.

Kicking your heels. No work to do.

Drummers. Trouser makers. A term of contempt used by jacket makers to describe trouser makers, because there is said to be less skill in making a pair of trousers. Trouser makers are also given the more contemptuous name of 'Four seams and a rub of soap'.

Board. Tailor's workbench.

Shears. Tailor's scissors.

Inch stick. Wooden ruler.

Baby. The stuffed pad of cloth that the tailor works his cloth on.

Dolly. A roll of material, wetted, and used as a sponge to dampen the cloth.

Mangle. Sewing-machine. The old machines were worked by a treadle, and looked more like mangles.

Banger. A piece of wood with a handle, used to draw steam out of the material during ironing. Makes the surface smoother.

Goose iron. Hand iron, which used to be heated on a naked gas flame. Tailors use electric irons now, and goose irons have largely gone out.

A skiffle. A fast job that the customer wants in a hurry.

A pork. A job that the customer rejects, but which can be sold to someone else. (From the Jewish attitude to pork, as untouchable).

A kill. A job that is no good at all, and cannot be resold, e.g., when a coat has been burnt with an iron.

Breeches Tailor

Some of the prestigious firms of West End tailors carry out only a small proportion of their work on the premises. Much of the work is given to 'outworkers', master craftsmen, contracted with one or other of the larger firms but working as self-employed craftsmen in their own premises. Some of these workrooms are extraordinarily modest and provide a striking contrast with the splendid showrooms of the tailoring firms. Until recently a seedy attic room in Newburgh

Street, Soho, was the workshop of an eighty-year-old tailor who has a reputation in the trade as the finest maker of riding breeches in the country.

Standing, Mr Head seems bent and stiff, but as soon as he has climbed up onto his table and is sitting cross-legged in the tailors' traditional lotus position, his appearance is transformed. Decades of work have made this crouched attitude natural, and his bones seem to have become bent into shape for it. With his legs crossed, the tailor's knees become his workbench and his bent neck brings his eyes close to his work. Mr Head stitches every seam by hand, with stitches so small that they are scarcely visible.

Older people particularly tend to become harassed by change, and feel insecure when their routine is disturbed. Like many craftsmen in London, Mr Head was disturbed by constant rent and rate rises and felt threatened by the redevelopment of the streets around him. As a self-employed man his time was more and more taken up with paperwork, for which he had no skill.

After sixty-six years as a London tailor, sixty of them with the same Savile Row firm, most men would be content to call it a day. But Mr Head has received an offer to join a small firm of craftsmen tailors in Yorkshire, with a cottage provided as part of the deal. He was very happy to accept, and so, at the age of eighty, one of London's finest tailors has left Soho to start a new career in the country.

Swordmaker

These days the 'conventional' weapons, rifles, tanks and so on, are of doubtful value in a war. Even more ineffectual is that most archaic of weapons, the sword. Nevertheless, swords are still being made in fairly large numbers in London. There are two main markets for them: officers in all three Services are required to wear swords on ceremonial occasions. Also there is a brisk demand from the theatrical profession for replicas of swords of all periods.

Joseph Starkey is the name of a small firm making swords for the services, and other military accessories too, in a mews workshop in South London. In the sword shop there are two young craftsmen who are proficient at all the different skills required for assembling a sword. The sword blade is made of steel, on which a decorative pattern has to be etched with acid. The hand-shield consists of several separate pieces of cast metal alloy which need to be brazed (soldered and hammered) together, and generally tidied up before it can be sent to an independent firm for gilding. The hand-grip of the sword is carved wood, and over this the craftsman stretches a covering of white sharkskin. The sharkskin, which comes from an uncommon Pacific species, is put on wet, so that when it dries it contracts and tightens over the hand-grip. A coil of gold wire around the sharkskin completes the decoration of the sword handle.

The same craftsmen make the leather scabbards that hold the swords. A ceremonial sword scabbard is made from the best quality heavy leather, which has been tanned by the traditional oak-bark process. The leather is worked while wet, cut into shape and sewn to make the basic shape. A steel core, only slightly larger than the sword blade, is pushed into the scabbard to hold it in shape as it dries. A protective tip of brass is fitted to the scabbard. This is the 'chape' and it is decorated with standard patterns which are chased (incised) into the surface with a sharp tool tapped with a hammer. Two brass lockets higher up on the scabbard are decorated in the same way.

At Joseph Starkey's the swords are made two at a time and together the two craftsmen produce an average of six swords in a week.

Swordstick Maker

Swordstick-making is a surprising trade to have survived so far into the twentieth century, but there is still a lively demand from tourists for swordsticks to take home as curios. Mr Drew works in the basement of James Smith's magnificent umbrella shop in New Oxford Street and divides his time between repairing umbrellas— anything up to 150 a day may come in during wet weather—and making swordsticks.

The sword in a swordstick is hidden in an elegant swagger stick of malacca wood, hickory or maple. Mr Drew drills a long hole through the stick, a job that requires great care because the hole must be absolutely straight so that the drill does not pierce or split the sides of the narrow stick. The swordblades are ready made, but Mr Drew makes the silver mounts himself, beating them up out of a flat sheet of silver. The silver mount acts both as a base for the sword and a decoration for the stick itself.

Shoemaker

The census of 1851 reveals that there were 38,000 shoemakers in London. It was by far the largest hand trade, and occupied about 2 per cent of the population. Some of the work was exquisite, judging from examples that have been preserved. Some ladies' shoes were sewn with 60 stitches to the inch; stitches so tiny as to be almost invisible. The shoemakers used to work by the light of a candle, with a bottle of water beside it acting as a lens to focus the light on the work.

Later in the century, shoes could be made entirely by machine, and there was a massive decline in the number of hand-craftsmen. Northampton became the capital of the industry, but in London a few hand-craftsmen carried on. Today there are two groups of customers who keep the craftsmen in business: the crippled and the very rich. People with deformed or injured feet must have their shoes specially made for them and there are a number of small firms of orthopaedic shoemakers who cater for this need. And for the others, who appreciate the luxury and comfort of a fitted hand-made shoe and who can afford to pay the price of it, there are just two or three firms in the West End who make bespoke shoes on the premises. A pair of 'London best' shoes may cost £120 or upwards, and delivery may take four months or so, but judging by the number of customers, the comfort and durability of the finest shoes justifies the expense.

Max Beerbohm in a letter of the 1950s asked a friend: 'Tell me, is Lobb still the best shoemaker in London?' Answering in the late 1970s we can still answer in the affirmative. Lobb's shop has all the plush grandeur that might be expected of a St James's Street shop. There are glass cases with showpieces like the first 'Wellington' boot, and Queen Victoria's tiny and much-used shoe last. But in spite of the red carpets and comfortable antique chairs there is a strong smell of freshly cut leather, and ranged around the stately reception room are the craftsmen's benches. Several of the directors of the firm are practising craftsmen. When a customer enters, one of the men at the benches puts down his work and takes off his apron to serve him.

At Lobb's several craftsmen deal with the different processes of making a pair of shoes. Not all of their employees work at St James's. Many are outworkers, working at home and only returning every so often to collect work. Lobb's even deliver work to some of their men, and there is a story of one Lobb outworker who joined the firm in 1892 and held the job for sixty years without ever visiting the premises again, although he lived only a sixpenny bus ride away.

First the customer's feet are measured and the measurements used to construct wooden models of his feet, the lasts. The fitter records every dimension of the feet minutely. Every bump and corn is charted so that when the last is made it will be a perfect model of that particular foot.

The craftsman who cuts out the leather for a shoe is known as the 'clicker'—(the name originates from the sound of the leather being cut). At least eight pieces of calfskin are used for the shoe upper. The clicker is the foreman shoemaker and he distributes the work among the other craftsmen. He passes the leather pieces to the 'closer' who trims them and sews them together, incorporating the linings.

The craftsman who finishes off the construction of the shoe by sewing on the sole and adding the heel is called the 'maker'. Traditionally the shoemaker sits at a very low stool, about 15 inches off the ground. He has a small bench in front of him, but most of the time he supports the work on his knees, holding it there with a gigantic elastic band called a stirrup, which passes under his foot. Shoemakers use a well-waxed thread which they make themselves from several thicknesses of hemp twine. The thread tapers towards the end and instead of using a needle, the shoemaker twists a pig's bristle on to the tip of the thread. He pierces holes in the leather with the sharp point of the awl, and guides the thread through the hole with the bristle.

The inner sole is soaked overnight and is moulded on to the last so that it makes a perfect fit. The upper is wrapped around the last, and fitted like a glove so that the tensions are even. Sewing on the welt comes next. This is the strip of leather on to which the sole is sewn. Finest cowhide is used for the sole. The heel is built up with strips of leather attached to the shoe with rivets. Nails are not used anywhere else in the shoe.

Lobb's customers range from pop stars to potentates. Some of them order shoes in unusual leathers like crocodile skin. One of the biggest problems for shoemaking firms these days is finding best quality leather. Leather tanned by the modern chemical process is not sufficiently long-lasting, and all shoemakers prefer to use leather tanned by the traditional oak-bark method.

Shoe Last and Tree Maker

The last and tree maker is an independent tradesman within the shoemaker's workshop. He is a woodworker in a world of leather craftsmen. His job is to carve wooden models of his customers' feet. The last is a wooden template around which the hand-made shoe is constructed. The tree is another model of the foot, made to fit into the shoe to keep it in shape.

The last maker has to carve an accurate replica of every bump and depression of the foot, working from a traced outline of the foot and a set of measurements. The arches of the sole, the corns and bony promontories are all faithfully reconstructed out of a single piece of wood. Not only does the work have to be accurate within a tiny fraction of an inch, but it must be elegant too. There is such a thing as an ugly last; it is a question of line. The elegance that the craftsman imparts to the last persists in the finished shoe. So the last-maker is not only a craftsman with the highest woodworking skills, he is a sculptor too, and his work is governed by aesthetic considerations.

Tom van Steenhoven makes lasts and trees for Lobb's of St James's. He is in his sixties and has been in the trade since he left school. He started work as a delivery boy at one of the many hand-made shoe firms and spent his first two years at work delivering boot-trees on the firm's tricycle: 'I had to wait to learn, because all the craftsmen were on piecework and couldn't spare the time to teach me.'

In the opinion of his colleagues there is not a last and tree-maker in the business who can approach the quality of his work. He sets such high standards that it would be almost impossible for a younger man's work to meet with his approval.

'People nowadays won't accept the old ways. They think that they can do better. But the old ways have been tried again and again and most of the time they are right. You get these young men making shoes now. They bang the tree into the shoe. "The tree will put the shoe into shape," they say. But how can it? The shoe is just an inanimate object. You are the man who should make the shoe fit properly, that's what I say.

I had this apprentice who said he was nervous working with me. "With me?" I said. "Look, I'm just an ordinary bloke." "It's what the boss said," he said. "You're the finest tree-maker in England." Well, that's mad. It's only that I'm a decent one among the two or three that's left. In the old days I would probably be well down the list.

Take a firm making trees today. There might be three men working and they'll produce fifteen pairs of trees a week. Well, I've just come across my work book and I found that in 1941 I was making 45 pairs in a week—that was just me on my own.

Now that I'm getting older I'm getting slower. But these young chaps, they'll never get quick. That is the difference in work in England today. You cannot conceive how we used to work. And we used to work willingly. Now they're only interested in the money. What kept you going was the feeling that it was your trade and you wanted to carry on with it.

You can't help worrying how standards have slipped. I haven't been to Russia and so I don't know about that. But I do know that this country is wrong when it allows the trades to die.'

Tom van Steenhoven is an inventive craftsman and he has managed to introduce new ideas to a trade that has hardly changed in centuries. His workshop is filled with little labour-saving devices that he has dreamed up. He has adapted shoe trees so that they can be made to flatten out a shoe, or enlarge it slightly to give a more comfortable fit, or to change the shape of the toe. Being a little rheumatic himself, he has carved himself a shoe horn two feet long so that he can put his shoes on without bending down. His prototype was taken up by the firm and they sell all he makes.

'All my ideas are a bit Heath Robinson, but they work. It's just cussedness I've got; other people wouldn't have the obstinancy.'

Lobb's keep all their shoe lasts, carefully labelled with each customer's name. As a customer's feet change with the years, his lasts are adapted with a little bit shaved off here, and a little extra padding there, so that each pair of new shoes is a perfect fit. The lasts are stored in racks in a large room below the shop. In the dim light, the room is like the catacombs, with grisly rows of feet in place of skulls. One of Lobb's employees, as the story goes, checks the obituary notices in *The Times* every day, and when the day of judgement comes for a customer, his lasts are finally removed from the racks.

PART VIII

Environmental craftsmen

The stone-carvers, signpainters, plasterers, glass painters have made their mark on the buildings of London, and the evolution of their crafts is part of the history of architecture. The architecture of our own day is governed by considerations of expense, and hand-craftsmanship is an expensive luxury. This presents a threat to these trades, more perhaps than any others.

Architectural Sculptor

Over the centuries the architectural sculptors have made a glorious contribution to the architecture of London. Take a stroll around the centre of the City and look up at the arches over the doors and windows, at the friezes and the decorative columns. There is scarcely a public building in London, built before, say, 1920, that was not embellished with some kind of carved decoration in stone. We do not know the names of most of the men who made these decorations but the work of our greatest architects would be incomplete without them.

When Wren was rebuilding St Paul's and the City churches after the Great Fire, there must have been literally hundreds of sculptors working on details of his grand designs. We give credit to one great man for these buildings, but the creative part of the architecture did not stop with him. Every carving is a sculptor's individual statement as well as being an integral part of the whole design. Architect and sculptor shared the same purpose and worked together as a harmonious team.

Today the relationship between architecture and sculpture has changed. Sculpture is still used to decorate modern architecture but it is not usually a necessary element in the overall design. When sculpture does appear it is usually applied to a building as an afterthought. So the tradition of architectural sculpture, which continued in an unbroken line from the Norman through the Gothic and the Classical to the Victorian carvers, has not been carried through into modern architecture. All the same, the tradition is very much alive. Nowadays the architectural sculptor is almost exclusively involved with restoration, but still his work is as creative as it has always been.

One of the finest practitioners of the trade, as well as being a teacher with a missionary's zeal for the old traditions, is Kenneth Gardner, foreman of the architectural sculpture studio at St Paul's Cathedral. Leader of a close-knit team of sculptors, he is engaged in the 'restoration'—in fact the total recarving—of many of the stone decorations of the cathedral that have been eroded by the combined effects of weather and pollution.

One of the most surprising things about Kenneth Gardner's skill is his ability to improvise in stone without making a preparatory drawing. Recarving the great decorative urns by Caius Cibber he aims to recreate the finished effect of Cibber's work without laboriously following all the details of the original sculptor's design. Mr Gardner is so well versed in the language of classical sculpture that he can design a rich billowing cornucopia of flowers and fruit as he goes along. What makes his achievement all the more incredible is the fact that a stonecarver can only subtract from a slab of stone and never add to it. When he seems to be building up a complex arrangement of shapes, it is an illusion, because he is actually working in reverse, whittling away the stone around the shapes until they are the only parts of the original stone that remain.

A feature of Mr Gardner's work is the rich variety of texture that he manages to impart to the stone:

'The stone itself is a dead material, you see. You've got to make it live. You see this area—it's not cleaned up. The tool cuts are left in and they give life to your carving. You draw with the tool all the time.

It's the same with the overall design. You get your contrasts by putting a fussy thing next to a plain one. Then you've got to think about constrasts of colours. In stone you have three colours. You have highlights, which catch the light. You have greys. And you have blacks, which are the shadows. Out of the stone you develop a contrast of colours. It's like painting in stone.

All the urns that I am doing are different. You don't laboriously copy a flower. You regard the thing as a whole job and put in what detail that you see fit. I haven't a clue what I'm going to put in; it just comes.

What I'm concerned about in this trade is the loss of tradition. You can count the pukka carvers on the fingers of one hand. I'm a third-generation sculptor myself. My father was an architectural sculptor and so was his father before him. So I grew up in the craft. Right through history there have been these connections following through.

I love to teach people. My thrill is to get the opportunity to teach someone. When I see a carver adopting my style, that's when it becomes delightful. It must be passed on from one man to the next. That's the only way to teach it. Unless someone can train you in the traditional way, there's no way to learn. It needs to be someone who exudes enthusiasm. You can't teach this in an art school; working in a studio like this is the only way to pick it up.

It's such painstaking work it brings out the right men in the end. Quality comes out, because it's not an easy job. What it boils down to is individual effort, pride in your work, experience, the right temperament—that's important, and willingness to take criticism from your fellow-men. You need patience too, but I think that comes with training. You know, the crafts are a luxury these days. What we need is a bit of luck and a few champions.

All our men are great to work with. There's a kind of comradeship in the studio that makes it a job in a million. You grow up with the chaps and become part and parcel of each other. It never gets easy; the last job is as difficult as the first. Every job has a different problem.

You know this job gives you an interest in other things in life that many people miss. You learn to see line and colour in other things. I even find myself looking at bus advertisements to see how well the lettering is spaced. Even on holiday you take a different attitude. You notice things that other people might not see. The chaps go to the sea for their holidays but now they stop off at Winchester and Salisbury to see the carving there. It all comes down to this job. There is so much more to it than stonecarving. It is a job in a million.'

Towards the end of 1975 the Dean of St Paul's announced that the funds for the cathedral's restoration had almost run out, and that the wages of the architectural sculptors could no longer be guaranteed. Although an appeal in 1973 had raised over two million pounds, the funds had run out before the work was completed. This raised a storm of protest. At present the work is continuing, but at a reduced speed. At stake is not only the restoration of one of London's most glorious buildings, but the continuity of one of London's proudest trades.

Model Maker

The architectural model-maker is usually asked to make a model of a building before it is put up. He has an architect's plans and scale drawings to work from. But Nicholas Gaffney is an unusual model-maker: he specializes in making models of buildings that have long since vanished. He works on slender evidence—an early drawing or watercolour of the place, or its ruins. His reconstructions demand a tremendous knowledge of period architecture and building techniques, as well as great skill in modelling the intricate architectural details on a tiny scale.

Working on a model of the Roman basilica that was covered when Leadenhall market was built in 1886, Gaffney's only source material was a series of contemporary black and white drawings. These had been made on the spot before the basilica was covered by the new building. From this fairly thin evidence, Gaffney has built an entirely convincing reconstruction which is destined for the London Museum. His model shows the ruins of the Roman walls as they were in 1886, the arches of a medieval building, and a nineteenth-century tenement house about to be demolished. The core of the model is built of wood, with a layer of plastic foam laid on top, into which the surface details of the reconstructed buildings are carved. Gaffney also uses a type of fine board made for watercolour painters; this material can be scored with a knife and painted to imitate the lines of tiles on a roof or the bricks of a wall. He builds up the worn and weathered colours of the masonry with paint sprays and watercolour. He delights in fine details like the peeling wallpaper and the sooty lines of the chimneys on the part-demolished house of his model.

Nicholas Gaffney is an 'amateur' in the original sense of the word, who does his work for the love of it. After a day's work in the studios of Thorps, the model-making firm, he goes home and starts work again. His own unpaid project is even more ambitious than any of the models that he makes commercially. For over two years, in his own time, he has been constructing a huge model of the great Abbey at Glastonbury. Only the incomplete ruins of the original Abbey remain, but Gaffney is rebuilding it in miniature with some of the dedication that possessed the craftsmen who produced the original. His attention to detail is prodigious. Each window is built out of several layers of cut card so that all the recesses of the masonry are reproduced.

Nicholas Gaffney is gifted with unusual concentration. 'When I concentrate I go into a sort of trance and I don't notice what's going on around me. If anyone wants me they usually have to shake me by the arm to attract my attention.'

Here is a craftsman who is lucky enough to earn his living at an occupation which remains, for most people who practise it, an enthralling hobby.

Architectural Decorator

In 1780 Robert Adam was looking for a way to make repetitive ornamentation for the ceilings, panelling and fireplaces that he was designing. Hand-carving was too expensive and time-consuming. A Swiss pastor had just invented a material called 'composition' which was soft like putty when freshly made, but dried out to form a hard and stable substance that could be painted to look like wood or plaster. While fresh and pliable it could be pressed into a mould and thus made to assume the shape of an elaborately carved ornament of wood. Adam bought the recipe for composition and entrusted the making of 'enrichments' with it to a London friend named George Jackson. Jackson's craftsmen carved moulds out of boxwood and the composition enrichments were cast from them. Today George Jackson's firm is still flourishing in London, and craftsmen there are still making composition and plaster enrichments from the same moulds that were carved for Robert Adam's original designs.

The names of the men who carved the boxwood moulds are unknown, but their achievement is breathtaking. It is difficult enough to carve a freestanding decorative relief, but these were carved in reverse, as depressions in a flat boxwood block. Somehow or other the craftsmen managed to carve the deeper areas of the design without damaging their work nearer the surface. Mr Cottee, who has been casting from these moulds all his working life, has never lost his wonderment at their craftsmanship: 'Where there are knots in the wood it just didn't seem to bother them. They carved into the lumps of boxwood just like that. The carving is unbelievable. I never cease to marvel at it. Even if you're used to it, you pull out a mould and you stand and look at it in amazement. You just don't believe it could be done.'

No less delicate than their composition enrichments for fireplaces, picture-frames and the like are Jackson's decorations in plaster. Here again they have a large stock of original plaster designs from which facsimiles can be cast. When commissions for totally new designs of plasterwork come their way, Jackson's modelling department produce the prototypes in clay. Mr Max Lewis is foreman here and he is adept at modelling abstract designs as well as decorative animals' heads and cornucopias of succulent fruits and flowers. A flexible negative mould of vinyl is made from the clay positive and from this any number of plaster casts can be made.

Another of Jackson's specialities is scagiola work. Scagiola is artificial marble, and as its name suggests it is of Italian origin. Many an Italian church has an echoing interior of scagiola. In England it is the prerogative of large banks, central libraries and municipal halls. In London the Fishmongers' Hall, the British Museum and Lancaster House are heavy with 'scag'. Wherever scagiola is to be found in England, the chances are that it was made by Jackson's Dan Phillips, or his father, or his grandfather . . . and so on back for over two hundred years. For the Phillips family have been in scagiola since it was first brought here from Italy. They have passed its secret recipe from father to son, jealously withholding it from outsiders. Now Dan Phillips and one other craftsman at Jackson's are the only people in the country who can make it.

The basic ingredients are straightforward—Keen's cement and good quality watercolour powders to colour it. But the proportions of the different colours are weighed out to a coded recipe. The colours are mixed into the cement by hand, to make a kind of plastic pudding. This is cut into slices and the different colours kneaded together to make the marbled patterns. 'The skill is in moulding with the hands what you can remember the marble looks like. It's a memory act. All we've got down on paper is the code.'

The marble-patterned scagiola is then cast, like plaster, in a mould, so that it can be used to make pillars, flat sheets or whatever shape is required. Once it has hardened, it is rubbed down with an abrasive stone and then oiled and polished. When it is erected on site, the finished scagiola is hard, shiny, beautifully patterned and virtually indistinguishable from the real thing. Sadly, though, these days it sometimes turns out to be more expensive.

Among the buildings that have been graced over the years with Jackson's decorations or restorations are the Palaces of Kensington, Lambeth and St James's, Brighton Pavilion, the Victoria and Albert Museum and Harvard University. But the firm is not only involved with the architecture of the past: their largest project in recent years has been the decoration of the complete interior of a vast summer palace for one of the Arab sheiks.

Grainer and Marbler

Here is a trade that has declined so much in recent years that even the finished product has become quite scarce. The grainer and marbler is a master of artifice. He uses paint to imitate the subtle grains and figures of the finest hardwoods and the colours and textures of the various types of marble. He can paint an ordinary door so that it seems to have been made from polished mahogany or walnut. He can make a sheet of hardboard look like the surface of rare marble. The grainer is the aristocrat of the house-painting trade. He used to be called in when decorating was almost complete to put the final finish on a job. His work was made to last and the best examples of graining and marbling can still be seen on Victorian and Edwardian shopfronts and in pubs and restaurants that have survived the 'developments' of the present century.

Oak, beech, walnut, mahogany, satinwood, teak—these are the principal woods in the grainer's repertoire. Each wood requires a different ground colour which is painted flat over the surface to be grained. Over this the grainer lays a coat of transparent colour, traditionally made with a powdered pigment mixed with a little beer. While this is still wet, he works it to imitate the texture of wood. He scratches into the wet paint and smears it with a cloth or feather to reveal the paler ground colour underneath. He pats the wet paint with a dry brush to create the little shadowed pores that are characteristic of some woods. He paints the curved and tapering lines of the wood grain with a sable brush. In all these processes he works at a tremendous speed to catch the paint before it dries. Finally, when his work is finished and dried, he covers it with a coat of varnish, which brings up the details he has painted, and protects his work for years.

At seventy-eight, Tom Clarke is a master grainer, who tries, against the odds, to maintain the high standards passed down to him by his father.

'My father set up on his own in 1870, just after he had served his apprenticeship. I think it cost £25 in those days to be an apprentice. I have got his indentures still—all on parchment—"I promise to be a faithful servant to my master over the five years of my apprenticeship," it says, all in copperplate handwriting. A grainer was something in those days, you know. There used to be a well-known grainer down the Borough. He had a horse and he had a groom to look after it. Now this painter had a job to do in Blackheath. In those days, from the Borough to Blackheath was like going into the country. So he rode to the job on his horse, in his tailcoat, accompanied by his groom. He rang the bell and told the maid, "I've come to grain the door." She went and told the lady of the house, and the message came back, "Tradesmen round the back." Oh my goodness, that done it. He was insulted. You see a grainer was much respected in those times. He was an important member of society.

A corner of the edge-gilder's workshop. The wooden press holds a batch of invitation cards, with gold leaf applied to one edge. At bottom left is the burnisher, which is tipped with a glass-smooth stone.

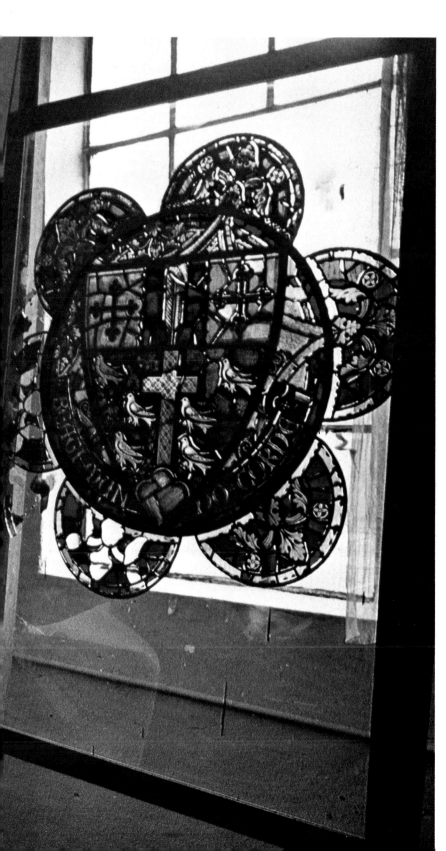

The stained glass painter. Each piece of coloured glass has already been cut to size. Now Bill Smith, the painter at Goddard and Gibbs studio, adds the darks and the lights. The cartoon for the finished window is draped over his bench and he paints each piece of glass in position on the cartoon (detail right). The iron oxide pigment is made permanent by firing in the kiln. The painter can also use acid to etch colour out of areas of the glass. The whole glass panel is just a fraction of the great rose window of Lancing College in Sussex.

Bespoke brushmaking. Mr
Ogilvie takes twenty minutes
to make a broom by hand,
but there are machines that
turn out six hundred in an
hour. Here the bristles are
secured with molten pitch.

Bespoke cameras. The
Gandolfi brothers of
Peckham make wood and
brass plate cameras to any
specification. Roughly a
fortnight's work goes into
each one. The Gandolfi's
are only the second generation
of a family firm that spans
nearly a century; their father
founded the business in
1880.

My Dad used to say, when you're representing wood, pick out the *best* bits of wood. If a carpenter's making a door or something, he'll always pick out the best wood. That's what we do too. I like to put plenty of figure into my work. The idea in graining is to make something that's really something and hits you in the eye. It's just the same with marbling. You always make marble to look effective. You don't copy it exactly. We always used to say that we tried to make marble not as it really is, but as it ought to be.'

Slightly different techniques are used for the graining and marbling of furniture. This kind of decoration has less bravura and is more realistic than exterior work. It is allied to *trompe-l'oeil* painting.

Signwriter

There is a permanent exhibition of the signwriter's art in every shopping street in London, and we are so familiar with the styles that we tend to walk past them without a thought. But John Edmett, whose family have been signwriters in Lamb's Conduit Street, Bloomsbury, for five generations, looks at signs with the critical eye of a professional:

'Do you know, twenty-five years ago we could have walked all over London and in every street I could have told you who made the signs. Every one had his quirks and his own way of doing things. We would all make up our own letters and adapt them for the particular shop that we were making them for.

I might be working on a simple job; well, I look at it and I think, now that wants a little something—perhaps a shade dropped in or a little flourish, just to relieve the thing. We don't get paid for these little details, but we can't leave it alone until it looks right.

A certain kind of person is compelled to take up this business for a kind of mental satisfaction. The only way to learn this sort of stuff is to work with craftsmen and ask them questions, why they do this, why they do that. And the only way to keep the craftsman's interest is by keeping the firm reasonably small, so that the people working there can see the complete thing. When you do it all yourself you get involved with the job. You lose yourself.'

In recent years the sign trade has become less personal, with many small firms closing down, and the large firms turning out mass-produced perspex signs with standardized graphics. Every signwriter used to be a one-man band, proficient at a wide range of skills. But the trade is becoming more specialized, broken down into departments so that in most firms one man designs a sign, another does the perspex parts, a third the metalwork. There is less involvement with the work: 'It becomes a kind of clockwatching activity, because there simply isn't the creative interest.'

There are not many signwriters left in London who can carry out the most testing work of the signwriter's repertoire—the painting and gilding of a glass sign. Shops and pubs of the Bloomsbury area still display magnificent examples of Edmett work of all different vintages. The signwriter paints on the back of the glass, and so he works blind—the lowest layer of paint, the undercoat, becomes the top layer when viewed from the front. The gold, in the form of gold leaf, is laid directly onto the back of the glass; often patterns are acid-etched into the glass to give the gilding added sparkle. A well-constructed glass sign will last for ever; its only enemies are vandals and redevelopment, both of which continue to take their toll of fine signs.

Stained Glass Maker

A stained-glass window is made up of small pieces of coloured glass held together by strips of lead. Like a coloured film the window transmits light and filters it into beams of separate colours. So a stained-glass window serves both to light and to decorate the interior of a building and the makers of a window have to reach a compromise between these two functions. A richly coloured and heavily painted window will transmit very little light. A window made of thinly coloured glass may allow a lot of light to pass, but the effect of the design may be weak and undistinguished.

A major window is usually made by a team of craftsmen, each one specializing in a different stage of the process. The designer is the overseer of the whole project. He prepares a coloured scale drawing of his design showing exactly how he wants the finished window to look. From the design a draughtsman prepares two full-size drawings of the window in black and white. The first is the 'cartoon', a charcoal or wash drawing that shows all the details of line and shading that will appear on the window.

The second full-size drawing is the 'cut-line' drawing which shows only those lines along which the different pieces of coloured glass will meet and be joined by leads. Planning the lead lines demands considerable skill and experience. The leads have both an artistic and an engineering function. The heavy black lines of the leads ought to contribute to the overall design of the window, and at the same time they need to be spaced in such a way that they give the maximum support.

The cut-line drawing is the blueprint by which the craftsman glass-cutter works. His job involves far more than simply cutting glass to size. He has to select the colours of glass that will be used from the vast range available. Even if adjacent pieces of glass are designed to be the same colour, the glass-cutter may select glasses of marginally different colours to provide contrast and to give life to the window. Laying his chosen glass on the cut-line drawing, the craftsman traces along the cut-line with a wheel cutter. Having cut a piece he sticks it loosely alongside its neighbours on a glass screen. This allows him to see how well the separate colours work together. He may have to change one or two pieces if the effect is not harmonious.

Now the loose pieces of coloured glass pass to the painter. There are three ways in which he can manipulate the glass to get a desired effect: he can stain the glass; he can paint it; and he can remove some of the colour from chosen areas of the glass by etching away the surface with acid. All these techniques are fairly limited. The only colour that can be stained into the glass is yellow. This is done by painting a silver compound onto the back of the glass and firing the glass in a kiln. The silver fuses with the glass to create an absolutely permanent stain. A beautiful range of yellows can be made in this way by varying the quantity of silver used.

The painting of stained glass is a form of enamelling. Coloured enamels are made by mixing metallic oxide pigments with powdered glass and water, painting it on, and firing the painted surface in a kiln. The technique does not give very colourful results — the enamelled glass is nearly opaque and an enamelled window transmits very little light. So the stained glass painter only paints the glass when he wants a dark, opaque tone and for this he uses only one colour, iron oxide, which gives a brownish-black. The painter follows the cartoon drawing as a guide and paints all the details of line, shadow and texture on to the coloured glass with iron oxide. Before it is fired the iron oxide paint behaves like watercolour and can be smeared onto the glass and scratched off or stippled to give a wide range of textures and effects.

Bill Smith is the glass painter at Goddard and Gibbs studios in Shoreditch:

'We call the foliage bits "the cabbage". As a young boy you start on the cabbage when you first come into the studio. Then you move on to a bird on a twig maybe. Then you do the drapery and you end up being allowed to do the faces. In the old days painters would specialize; you'd have drapery painters and flesh painters. Take Kent's work: if you look at all the faces you'll see that they're all brothers and sisters — because they were all painted by the same artist.

I came here by accident. I got cheesed off with the job that I was doing. Someone said are you interested in drawing? I said yes. I didn't even know that this trade existed.

You get to know the effect of your colours and you work accordingly. White light expands and fills out the space around it. Blue expands too, but red contracts. You've got to get the balance right. When the glass is fired you lose about 25 per cent of the density of the pigment; you have to make allowances for that.

The designer gets all the fame and credit. But there's always a painter in the background, beavering away.'

The stained-glass studios have been through lean years recently, with the declining patronage of their traditional clients, the Church. One major studio at the Whitefriars glass-works closed down recently. Nevertheless the art schools continue to turn out stained-glass designers in increasing numbers. In a trade where there are too many chiefs (designers) and not enough Indians (craftsmen) a few enterprising graduates have set up their own studios where they construct windows of their own design.

Candle Maker

The Roman Catholic Church has kept alive the traditional hand craft of candle-making on a commercial level by its rule that candles used in churches must be hand-made, and, what is more, made from beeswax. So in one corner of the highly mechanized factory of Prices Patent Candle Company there is a single craftsman making candles in a manner that has not changed since the monks of the Middle Ages used to make their own candles by hand.

Until recently every Church candlemaker had to be a Roman Catholic and the candles had to contain 95 per cent beeswax. But the rules have been relaxed and, as the cost of the wax has soared, decrees from Rome have allowed progressive amounts of cheaper additives to be used with the beeswax. The percentage of required beeswax went down to 65 and then to 51. It now stands at 25 per cent, and the remainder is made up from paraffin wax and stearin.

The principle of candle-making is simple: the candle wicks, made of cotton, are suspended from hooks over a pan containing hot liquid wax. The candle-maker scoops up some wax in a ladle and pours it down the wick from the top. As he pours he twists the wick with his left hand so that the wax flows evenly and a thin layer is deposited all round the wick. The layer gets rather thicker at the bottom than at the top since the wax cools slightly as it goes down. This process, known as 'casting the wax' is repeated over a hundred times so that the candle is built up from many concentric rings of wax. When a hand-made candle is cut through, these rings show up like the annual rings in the trunk of a tree.

A candle cannot be made in one continuous session since each layer of wax has to cool and harden before the next is added. Only two pourings or 'casts' are made at a time before the candle has to be put aside to cool. The making of a particularly thick candle might be stretched out over three weeks.

The wax has to be the right temperature or disasters can happen. If hot wax is put on before the lower layers have cooled, the whole lot may slide off the wick. This may not happen immediately, but after two or three days when the weight of wax has built up on the wick. The danger is even greater in the summer; during a heat wave the wax may never cool down properly and there is always a risk that it will slide off. To prevent this a wick is always knotted at the bottom, and sometimes the lid of a jam jar is strung on to provide a wide base on which the wax can rest.

The candles are finished off on a wooden bench. The bench and the tools are swilled with water, which acts as a lubricant. First the candle, still warm from the final casting with hot wax, is rolled on the bench with a flat rolling board. The craftsman pushes down with the full strength of his forearm until the candle is perfectly flat and smooth. Next comes the tipping. The gently tapering tip of a candle is made with the simplest of tools, which consists merely of a flat piece of wood with a rounded edge. The craftsman holds the edge against the top of the candle and rolls the candle beneath it. The wood digs into the warm wax, up to the wick. He chops off the excess candle at top and bottom by rolling the candle underneath the blade of a knife, held vertically, and the job is done.

Carpet Maker

Robert Wallace is a young Californian craftsman who designs fine modern carpets and wall hangings and makes them by hand with his own adaptation of a traditional hand-tufting technique. He found an eighteenth-century carpet-tufting tool in a junk shop in New York; the dealer did not know what it was, but Robert Wallace recognized it and used it as a basis for a tool that he developed and updated himself. His tufting tool is still hand-operated but it speeds up considerably the process of tufting a carpet.

Robert Wallace works with a couple of assistants in a converted smithy near Smithfield market. From here they send out carpets to decorate floors as far apart as the Stratford Hilton and the King of Nepal's Palace at Katmandu.

The carpets are made on a foundation of cotton material which is stretched on a frame and held vertically like an artist's canvas. He tufts with pure wool, dyed to his own specifications. He works on the back of the material, but moves to the front at intervals to see how the work is progressing.

The outlines of the design are drawn up on the material, but often he works freely, improvising as he goes along like a painter, working loosely in the seemingly intractable medium of woollen tufts. The tufting tool pushes loops of wool through the meshwork of the cotton; later the loops are sheared, by hand, to separate the two strands. Finally, when the whole work is finished, a rubber solution is laid down on the back of the carpet to hold the tufts permanently in place.

For his wall hangings, Robert Wallace shears the tufts to different lengths so that the final design is three-dimensional. When the hanging is lit from the side, a pattern of shadows appears which complements the coloured pattern of the original design.

Most of Robert Wallace's clients come to him direct with their commissions and some are introduced by a firm of interior decorators. A few works are made 'on spec' but these are very quickly sold.

PART IX

Instrument makers and glassworkers

Thomas Tompion, the greatest London clockmaker of them all, started out as a blacksmith. This emphasizes how the metalwork trades in London turned towards precision work. The precision craftsmen of London are centred round the Clerkenwell area. Here each specialist depends upon the service of the others. Together the community of independent craftsmen provides a fund of skills by which complex instruments can be built up. If any one of the trades declines, then the circle is broken. The only way the work gets done is for the craftsman to take on the work that his supplier used to do. An extreme example of this effect is Frederick Gandolfi, the camera-maker. One by one his suppliers dropped away and so he was forced to learn their skills himself.

Watchmaker

The waistcoat came into fashion in the eighteenth century at just the right time to accommodate the newest refinement of the clockmaker's art—the pocket watch. A gentleman was not considered well-dressed without an elegant gold timepiece upon a chain across his paunch. In today's fashions the waistcoat has declined although some men still wear the garment to provide a home for a horological heirloom. And there are about ten individuals in the world whose waistcoats carry heirlooms of modern times—pocket watches made within the last ten years by George Daniels of London.

As far as he is aware, George Daniels is the only man in the world making pocket watches professionally. His name is known from New York to Geneva and from Paris to Tokyo, but his huge reputation is based upon a total output to date of a mere dozen watches. His maximum output is one watch per year, and each watch involves between 2,000 and 3,500 hours' work. He makes every part himself, and does not duplicate the parts from one watch to the next. Each watch begins as a technical idea and in each work George Daniels has introduced a mechanical innovation or a refinement of an existing device. His output can be seen as a progression, each watch being an advance on the one before: 'The truth is that I've never been wholly satisfied with anything that I've done. After you've made a watch you can always see ways in which you could have done it better.

'I'd like to go down as a man who made a contribution to the long history of clockmaking. My duty, as I see it, is to produce a watch that will run for ten years without requiring any attention. Most pocket watches have to be treated as delicate scientific instruments that have to be handled very carefully. But I make mine for civil use; you can even drop them and they will not break.'

Mechanics and aesthetics are the twin inspirations behind a Daniels watch. His watches are required not only to perform unprecedented mechanical feats, but they must look superb as well.

'Of course the most important thing is how the watch works, but if it's not beautiful as well then it's useless. If a thing is not human it would not have any value for me.'

On the face of it, a Daniels watch is simplicity itself. A plain white face is usually subdivided into two, three or four dials; one for the hours and minutes, one for the seconds, with a press-button release that takes the hand back to zero, sometimes a temperature dial, and always a dial to indicate whether the watch needs winding. The backs of the watches are mechanically engraved with simple abstract patterns. Inside, the complexity of the watches' movements and the rhythms of their actions create their own intricate designs. Beauty and function are the same thing. George Daniels keeps decoration to a minimum. His eighteenth-century precursors often decorated the moving parts of their watches, even the hidden parts, with engraved designs. But here the movements are left plain, apart from the stark inscription: Daniels, London.

George Daniels watch movements are created to compensate for the weaknesses and irregularities that are inevitable in the traditional mechanisms. His contribution to date has been to design an escapement that does not need oil and does not vary with temperature or with the angle at which the watch is held. In some of his watches the central part of the movement itself rotates once a minute and this compensates for any variations in the angle at which the watch is held. Some actions are duplicated, so that a variation in one direction will be compensated by an equal change in the opposite direction. A well-conceived watch mechanism has the same kind of elegance as a neatly resolved mathematical equation.

'It's in the escapement that the beauty of the mechanism lies. This is where the poetry of motion gets into one. You can sense good proportions in an escapement. The right parts are the right shape for the work that they do.'

There are several conditions required for a revolutionary development in a scientific craft such as watchmaking. The development of new materials and advanced equipment can lead to mechanical innovations. Financial reward is a vital stimulus. The most important factor above all is the inventiveness of the craftsman himself. These factors have all contributed to George Daniels's success: his whole life has been directed towards the attainment of the right conditions for his inventive talent to thrive. When he first left school in the East End of London he became an errand boy, and not an apprentice watchmaker, as the wages were so much better; but his initiation as an errand boy made it easy for him to get on with people, in his opinion an important asset to a craftsman. George Daniels made himself financially secure before he embarked upon making watches by a highly successful career in watch restoration, which also served as a kind of apprenticeship in the methods of the masters. Now he works part-time as an expert adviser to Sotheby's, a position that brings a regular income as well as a continuing contact with fine watches of the past. His self-made financial independence gives him freedom to experiment, to take risks, and to spend time on a problem. He will even refuse to sell his work if he feels so inclined. His motivation is from himself, and he will not accept commissions: 'If I don't sell it, it doesn't matter to me. If a fellow is a good recipient, I might sell it to him. I had one client who asked if he could have his own name around the dial in place of the numbers. But I wouldn't do it and he took my point. I told him that he wasn't going to live for ever, and what was the use of a watch with his name on it after he had gone? I regard it as a client's duty to pay for a piece of work that the craftsman chooses to make, and to patronize the arts in this way.'

Considering the complex structure of a watch, it is surprising how much improvisation can go into the making of it. George Daniels starts by making drawings in which the positions of the main parts of the movement are roughly sketched out and the important angles calculated. But once he has started to make the watch he invariably deviates from his plans.

'I am an opportunist. I know roughly what I want a watch to look like, but my ideas develop as I go along. I can never anticipate exactly how a watch will turn out.'

He tends to work in long bursts of intense activity. When he is working on a watch he starts at 6.30 a.m. and carries on until late at night. 'I have to do things passionately. I don't like work and so I work twice as hard as anyone else to get it over and done with. More than anything else I would like to be riding through the Yorkshire Dales on my motor-bike.'

It is a disappointment to George Daniels that there are no young craftsmen making pocket watches. Although he has worked alone all his career, he is determined to spread his enthusiasm to a new generation of watchmakers. 'My job will be to make people leap the chasm and do creative work.' His ambition is to start a small school in London so that eventually London will be recognized once again as the world centre for technical innovation in watchmaking. Already by his own work he has put London back on a map that has been dominated for the last century and more by Swiss and then American and Japanese developments.

Clock Dial Painter

E. C. Longcluse paints and restores clock dials for many of the clockmakers of Clerkenwell, and his father did the same before him. Really he is a kind of specialist sign-painter. He is an expert at restoring the worn-down dials of old grandfather clocks; some have brass fittings that need to be polished and hammered back into shape; others have little decorative paintings that may need touching up—a rising sun, a bowl of flowers, cherubs, rural scenes. But his main task is the repainting of the numbers and clockmaker's name on the clock dial. He traces what remains of the original dial onto a sheet of paper and draws in the missing parts. He retraces the design onto the dial and repaints the whole thing with sign-painter's oil paint. He is absolutely open-minded about the paint he uses; he tries out anything new, and on a cheap dial he sometimes uses Letraset lettering, or he may print the dial with silkscreen.

This is the craftsmanship of improvisation. Every job is different and presents new problems.

Barometer Maker

A fine barometer has to be a beautiful piece of furniture as well as a precise scientific instrument. The barometer case calls upon the combined skills of the cabinet-maker, the marquetry-cutter and the French polisher, the inner workings demand the craftsmanship of the glass tube maker and the dial-painter. Assembling the parts of a barometer and checking its accuracy is a separate craft in itself. There are barometer-makers who carry out all these processes on their own: Bill Marney, who runs the firm of Garner and Marney on the edge of Clerkenwell, has all the skills at his fingertips, but much of his time is spent getting together a group of specialist craftsmen to deal with the various processes separately. Mr Marney's firm restores up to four thousand antique barometers in a year and makes a wide range of reproduction clocks as well as barometers.

A perfectionist in every detail, Mr Marney uses only the best part of each piece of wood for his cases. In a sheet of flame mahogany veneer, for instance, the best figure of the grain, known as the 'flame', appears at the centre. Another craftsman might be content to use the flame figure on the front of a barometer case and to use the less decorative part on the sides. Not Mr Marney. On his barometers and clocks, two or even three sheets of veneer are used on a single case so that the sides as well as the front are made only from the very best wood.

There are always young people in Mr Marney's workshops, learning the trade from him. He is a great campaigner in the cause of keeping the crafts alive in London, and he is an ardent supporter of the Clerkenwell Green Association for craftsmen, which is raising funds to enable master craftsmen to take on apprentices.

'When you teach a lad, it's no good forcing him. If they don't take to it they'll go away. I have to teach them everything—putting the instruments together, polishing and so on. For the first six months they don't earn their wages but I have to pay them all the same.

In this area we all work along with each other. Here you know all the craftsmen and we give each other work.'

Mr Marney's far-sighted policy of training young people has its gloomy side. In one year alone he lost six of his best young craftsmen. The mobility of the population makes it increasingly difficult for the trades to sustain their continuity.

Camera Maker

The techniques of photography have changed so much in recent years that it seems incredible that there is still a firm in London making mahogany and brass cameras of the kind that were used before the miniature camera was invented. The Gandolfi family have been making these cameras since 1880 and they have never stopped. Out of the original family of seven, there are only two Gandolfi brothers still working, both past retirement age but both determined to carry on. The demand for their work is greater than ever. There is a two-year waiting list, made up largely of young photographers.

There are very fine modern metal plate-cameras on the market, but the very existence of the Gandolfi cameras creates their own demand. Quite simply more beautiful cameras have never been made. As a violin does, a beautifully made instrument inspires fine work by the user.

A Gandolfi camera has a framework of wood, usually mahogany but sometimes teak, extending leather bellows, and brass screws and fittings. It is an extraordinarily versatile instrument in which every part has been designed to give the greatest number of variables. The front of the camera can be raised or lowered on its brass mount or swivelled at an angle. These movements are a means of adjusting the perspective of the picture. The back of the camera can be altered to give a vertical or a horizontal picture, and different backs can be used so that the size of the plates can be varied. The camera closes up to make a deceptively simple-looking mahogany box. Every camera is made to the specification of the customer. One of the greatest of the Gandolfis' skills is the ease with which they adapt their design to suit a particular requirement.

The versatility of the Gandolfi cameras is matched by the versatility of the craftsmen who make them. They start with thick mahogany boards and sheets of brass, and carry through all the processing of these materials themselves. They even have to make some of the special screws that are needed, as the last source of supply has dried up. The only parts that they do not make are the thin leather bellows. Perfectionism shows in every detail. Just one example—the screws that are visible on the finished camera are set in so that their grooves are all parallel.

The elder of the two brothers, Frederick Gandolfi, has a strictly regulated work routine:

> 'When I start a job I like to stick to it all day and see it right through. If the phone goes or if somebody calls, you break off, and before you know where you are it's midday. That's why it's sometimes useful to be deaf. I can switch off my hearing aid and I'm in a world of my own. I just love working. It's nothing to do with the money. It's a joy to come over to the workshop here and potter around.
>
> Someone asked me the other day how many cameras I make in a week. Well,

the question ought to be the other way round; how many weeks to make a camera. If I worked at one at a time I'd take about two weeks over each camera. But we do things in batches. The wood is cut on the machine saw and piled up on this shelf to mature a bit. The next stage is the joining; there are some of the joined pieces on the next shelf. Then it goes through for finishing and polishing. I do all the brasswork upstairs. Everything is done on a system.

Did you know that there are three hundred brass screws in a camera? In fact it was the camera-makers who set the brass screw people on their feet. I find that I don't need to draw out my measurements any more, or work from a plan; I've got it all in my head. If a customer wants a different format, I just add half an inch all round or whatever he wants.

In 1980 it will be a hundred years since my father started this firm. He started up on his own because he got the sack from another firm of camera-makers. And do you know why? Because he was working too hard and making too much money.

Things were tough in those days. My father left school and started work when he was twelve. In those days people used to work hard to survive. It's not like that now. They pay you to be lazy. That's the trouble with the social services. They make things so easy that they take all the drive out of a man.

My father was forty when I was born. There were seven of us in the family and we were well spaced out—that's how the business has kept going. We did have some hard times, between 1925 and 1935. That's when all the other camera-makers went out of business. It was hard on the small firms then, but somehow we just kept going.

It's getting hard on the small firms again now. The Government don't allow you any peace of mind. All the red tape and bureaucracy that's attached to this kind of work. They are clobbering the little man.

All this publicity may lead to something good, I don't know. The last time the television people came they were here three days. They paid me for the time it took, yes, but it's not the money I want. It's my time that is precious to me. That was three days of life wasted as far as I was concerned.

All the same it does bring a bit of satisfaction. When the last film was on TV a lady in this street came up to me and said, "I saw your show last night, Mr Gandolfi, and you've done us proud." It made me feel I'd done something for the street. I felt good about that.'

Glass Maker

Glassmaking must be the only spectator craft. It is certainly the only craft trade in London where the public are encouraged to come and watch. At the Whitefriars glass works in Harrow there is a guided tour every day. The craftsmen at work provide a continuous display of intricate and balletic movements, manipulating the molten glass on the end of their blowing irons like syrup on a spoon, twisting it, swinging it, rolling it and blowing it, passing it from one to another. They move together with a rhythm and precision that is a joy to watch. Everything has to be done at speed while the glass is hot. With years of practice the master glassmakers make instant decisions and work with such rapid and economical movements that the whole process looks like a well-rehearsed ritual dance.

The glasshouse is about the size of a small aircraft hangar, and unbearably hot. Roaring in the centre of it are two massive furnaces containing pots of molten glass. Scattered around the perimeter of each furnace, just out of range of the red glow, are several small huddles of activity, groups of five or six men working together as a team.

Within each team there is a clearly defined pecking order. Seated in solitary state and remaining relatively still and cool is the head of the group called suitably enough the chairman or 'gaffer' (chairman because he sits on the glassmaker's chair). His is the least strenuous work, but the most skilled. He puts the finishing touches to the glass, shaping the handle of a glass tankard, for instance, or uniting the stem and foot of a wineglass.

The gaffer is served by one or two or more junior craftsmen called 'servitors'. The servitors make the basic shapes of each piece. Their work involves blowing the glass, sometimes judging the correct shape by eye, but more often blowing the glass into a mould. The mould is opened and closed with the foot.

In turn the servitors are served by the most junior craftsmen of all, the footmakers. Their job is to draw gobs of molten glass from the batch in the furnace, carefully judging the correct quantity. Then they roll the glass on a smooth iron slab (this is called marvering), to ensure that it is of an even consistency. As in most structured societies it is the man on the bottom of the scale who has the hardest conditions. The footmakers spend their day stripped to the waist and sweating under the fierce heat of the furnace.

Mr Baxter, the chief designer at Whitefriars, points out that the most astonishing skills of the craftsmen are best shown when a new design is tested.

'All the first trials are made by eye without any moulds. The craftsman is simply working from a drawing and he invents the way of making the piece as he goes along. It is incredible how the skilled man can pick up exactly the right amount of glass and get all the shapes right the first time.

We do have people here whose families have been glassmakers for several generations. The family tradition still means something, but it's on its last legs. People don't follow on from their fathers any more. They make up their own minds. At one time the glassmaker was a very respected member of the community. You were one of the craftsmen and people looked up to you. But now you're just regarded as someone working in industry.'

The Whitefriars Company started on the Embankment near the Temple, where it was already established in 1680. Traditionally, glasshouses never extinguish their fires. When, in 1920, the firm moved up to their present factory at Harrow, they took a burning brazier from the original furnace to ignite the new one. So the flames of their furnaces have been burning continuously for nearly three hundred years.

Glass Engraver

An engraving on glass is the most subtle and elusive image. Look at it in certain lights and it is nearly invisible. Direct the light source differently and the image sparkles with light. In this respect it resembles the earliest kind of photograph on glass, the daguerrotype, which comes to life only when it is held against a black backcloth.

The glass engraver can interrupt the transparency of the glass by two distinct techniques. In wheel engraving flat areas of glass are ground off the surface with an abrasive wheel. But the most delicate effects are achieved with stipple engraving, in which the craftsman builds up an image out of tiny opaque dots on the surface of the glass made with gentle taps of a diamond-pointed tool.

Alec Cobbe is a stipple engraver who took up the craft as a hobby after seeing museum examples of seventeenth and eighteenth-century Dutch engraving. He might still be regarded as an amateur in as much as he earns the bulk of his living at another job, but if quality is the criterion, then he is a professional. He specializes in engravings of houses and landscapes and every piece of work is commissioned.

Alec Cobbe starts by taking panoramic photographs of his subject, and then works out the composition by making small preparatory paintings. When engraving, he works in a darkened room, with a single light source bounced off a mirror on the table on to the glass. The image appears incredibly slowly from a myriad of tiny dots, each dot creating a tiny star of light. Unworked areas loom as dark silhouettes in contrast with the sparkling areas of dots. 'That's why it's so good doing skies; the clouds hold the light in the same way that the glass does.'

Robert Wallace hand-tufts his carpets from the back and only comes to the front at intervals to inspect his work. This piece is to be a wall-hanging and the tufts are cut to different heights so that the light creates shadows that contribute to the overall design.

Michael Holt, at Price's, hangs up a hoop of embryo Church candles. They are made by pouring molten wax down the wicks, gradually building it up in thin layers.

Richard la Trobe Bateman's home is furnished
with his own chairs. His furniture is highly
personal, elegant but robust.

The copperplate printing presses at Thomas
Ross weigh up to two tons and have been in
constant use for a hundred years. Here the
printer is lifting a printed proof off the plate.

Joe Cunnah, one of the partners at the boat-
building firm of George Sims and Sons, uses
a string to check that the ribs of his boat are
in line. If the skeleton of a boat has a good
even line then the boat should move well in
the water. This boat is for an eight-man crew
and will take about six weeks to build.

The elegant face of a pocket watch by George Daniels. The smaller round dial shows the seconds, while the quadrant dials show temperature (left) and whether the watch needs winding (right). The temperature dial is a pleasant luxury, but mechanically super-fluous, because George Daniels' watch movements are compensated for temperature changes.

The movement of a George Daniels watch. Every part is made by Daniels himself and each watch takes between 2,000 and 3,500 hours to complete. 'The most important thing is how the watch works, but if it's not beautiful as well then it's useless.'

A Clerkenwell clockmaker. This district has been a centre for the clock trade for centuries and there is still a concentration here of specialists and their suppliers. In communities like this, craftsmen tend to become mutually dependent, each one providing a specialist service for the others.

Between 600 and 800 hours' work go into a 'London best' shotgun, made by John Wilkes and his craftsmen in Soho. (Right) The gun stocks are 'checkered' with a traditional pattern of criss-cross lines.

The craftsman in the workshop (below) is holding a gun with a curved stock, made for a right-handed sportsman with a dominant left eye. The rough piece of walnut in the vice at the right is being carved to make a stock.

The glass engraver, Alec Cobbe, creating a portrait of a country house on glass, by stippling with a diamond-pointed tool. The glass vessel was made at the Whitefriars glassworks to his own specification.

Cut glass at Whitefriars. The patterns are cut into the wine glasses with a revolving carborundum stone, cooled with water. The craftsman makes each cut with one slow and steady sweep against the stone. It looks easy but it takes years to learn to control.

The job of the 'servitor' at the Whitefriars glassworks is to prepare the glass by 'marvering' or rolling it on a smooth metal table. He then gives it a preliminary blow before passing it on to the next member of the team.

Mick Martin, of Giddens, assembling a saddle. With an expensive raw material, one of the craftsman's skills is to make economical use of the leather, and every spare bit is saved for possible use later.

John Duffield is well past retiring age, but he has no trouble creating a 70-lb. tension on the strings of a tennis racket. The metal bar spanning the length of the frame is called the 'billiard' and is put there to prevent the frame buckling under the strain.

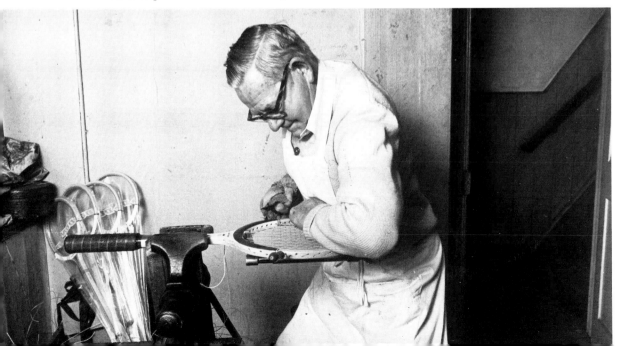

Most of his engraving is done on goblets of his own design which are made for him at the Whitefriars glassworks. But he is beginning to question the tradition of engraving on a glass vessel of some kind. 'I've become thoroughly dissatisfied with putting a house on a glass vessel. Why a vessel? The problem is that if you have a flat piece of glass you have got to think what to mount it on. The shape of the glass is the dominant thing. The object has a stronger presence than the image that is engraved on it. A glass engraving is not robust enough to stand up to all the other visual things in a room. It does not project itself. You have got to *decide* to look at it.

'This is why I'm working on the idea of making small engravings, enclosed in little boxes with built-in light sources. When you open the box you commit yourself to looking at it. It's like a book. When you open a book you exclude everything else in the room and focus your attention on reading it.'

The art of glass engraving is going through something of a revival today; this is partly due to the example and influence of Laurence Whistler who first used the technique to illustrate his own poems in 1935. By its very nature stipple-engraving is a small-scale craft, but Laurence Whistler, who lives and works in Dorset, has managed to adapt it for large-scale work. With the help of an electrically operated drill he has made engravings for sizeable church windows with great success.

PART X

Sports and games

Sports equipment provides a rich range of work for the craftsman. Guns, saddles, cricket bats, racing boats—they can all be made to measure for the discerning sportsman. The tremendous surge of popularity of sports of all kinds has meant that it pays large firms to take up sports equipment manufacture. Machine production has eclipsed the craftsmen in several trades, but still the best equipment is made by hand.

Gunsmith

London has been the capital of the gunmaking trade for centuries and all over the world the finest shotguns are still described as 'London best'. A 'London best' shotgun is specially fitted for a customer like a suit of clothes or a pair of shoes. Before work is started on a gun the client is taken to the shooting grounds for a fitting. Every shooting man has his own idiosyncrasies of sight and technique. You fire a shotgun with both eyes open; with some people the right eye is dominant, with others the left. The wooden part of the gun, the stock, is carved to a shape that suits the client's eyesight. A right-handed man with a dominant left eye needs a stock with a kink in it so that when he brings the gun up it is the left eye that follows the line of the barrel. Left-handed, cross-eyed—however a customer is made, the gunmaker can fit up a gun to suit him.

The gunmaker has to be master of a wide range of craft skills. He is metalworker, blacksmith, woodcarver rolled into one. Lock, stock and barrel, all the parts of a gun are finished and fitted by hand. Most gunmakers buy in their steel gun barrels from an outside firm, but the final boring of the barrel is done by hand. The parts that make up the action of the gun are usually roughly pre-cast at an outside foundry, and filed and finished off individually by the gunmaker.

The stock is carved by hand from a block of well-seasoned walnut. The art of stocking (making a stock) is to carve out a space for the gun's action so that every screwhead and projection fits exactly with no gaps between the metal parts and the wood. As much wood as possible is kept, to give the stock maximum strength.

The London gunmakers finish off their work with a traditional style of decoration that gives the gun a marvellous finish. The stocks are decorated with a criss-cross pattern of engraved lines known as 'checkering'. Checkering is put on with a three-cornered file that the gunmaker makes for himself. The exposed steel of the gun is engraved with an intricate abstract pattern of scrolls and swirling lines.

The firm of John Wilkes in Soho was established in 1830, but the Wilkes family had already been making guns for some time before that. The present John Wilkes is the fifth generation as head of the firm with the same name. He works with two assistants, building his own new guns and restoring the older guns of other London makers.

'We had a customer who came in one day and said "Look, this gun is misfiring; I can't understand it, my grandfather never had any trouble like this."

I said, "Oh yes, and how is your grandfather?"

He said, "Him? He's been dead these fifty years."

That's one of the pitfalls of the gun trade. They are so good that they last for three or four generations.

When a man comes through the door I can usually tell what he wants; whether he's a rifle or a pistol man; or whether he just wants to know the way to Oxford Circus.

When you talk of an old gun you're talking about before the First World War. The mechanics of gunmaking were worked out by then and have hardly changed since. You get shorter barrels and little details like that, but the essentials haven't changed.

At the most there must be two hundred men now making guns by hand in this country. Fifty or sixty years ago there would have been five or six thousand. You never used to see imported guns in those days. The Lord of the Manor might buy his gamekeeper a cheap Belgian gun maybe, and replace it after three years. Now there are many more foreign guns creeping in.

With restoration work it's easier to deal with the best quality guns than the cheaper ones, because they were made right in the first place. The cheaper ones were botched from the start and you've got to botch them to get them working again.

Most of the tools that you see here we have made ourselves. We might need a special tool to get into a particular space; we make that tool and it might not be needed for another twenty years. The tool gets put down on the workbench and it isn't used again until another gun comes in with the same problems. All the time we're adapting old tools. We get a file, say, bend it in the fire, re-harden it and use it for a particular job. The next gun might need something totally different.

We're having a bit of trouble with the rent and the rates just like everyone else. But if people can get the Government to change their minds about big schemes like Piccadilly then I think they should be able to do something for small firms like us. About seventy-five per cent of our work is exported.'

Taxidermist

Business is brisk for London taxidermists. There are a surprising number of hunters who want to hang evidence of their prowess on their dining-room walls, whether their specimens were bagged on safari in Africa, India or nearer home on the Sussex Downs. At any English foxhunt the Master may present mask, brush and pads of the kill to the hunt followers who have kept up with the hounds, and they like to have them mounted as mementos of the occasion.

Fishermen are good clients too, and the monsters that do not get away often find their way to the taxidermist's table. From time to time the curators of zoos and wildlife parks choose to have their prize specimens mounted when they die; some of these end up as museum exhibits. There is even a lively domestic trade from bereaved pet lovers who cannot bear that final parting with their favourite parrot or poodle.

The taxidermist is a kind of divine sculptor, seeming to breathe life into a model of an animal by clothing it in the dead creature's skin. The taxidermist needs to have a broad knowledge of animal behaviour so that he can set his specimens in convincing attitudes, and he must be as dispassionate as a butcher about cutting up their bodies. What is more, he needs a flair for sculpture and painting, as many of the details of a mounted specimen have to be created out of plaster and paint.

Archie Henderson is a young taxidermist at the London taxidermy studio in Hackney. When he came to London from Scotland a few years ago he already knew how to preserve skins and mount specimens.

'My father was the local poacher, so I always had plenty of animals to practise on. I used to keep ferrets and all sorts of animals myself.

My mates don't quite understand it. They're down at the pub by six in the evening, and I'm still working at eight. A skin won't wait, you see. If you leave it, it'll rot away. If a skin comes in and it needs doing, I'll come in at any time. I'll work all night on it if necessary.

Skinning the big stuff is difficult. It's tiring on the arms and fingers. We skinned an elephant once. We were moving around a ton and a half of meat. My God, it stank. I stank for about a week, and I used to have a series of baths every day.'

One lion-skin arrived in twenty-five pieces which had to be carefully sewn together. The skin of a bird is delicate, and it is difficult to remove it in one piece without tearing it. Care must be taken with some fish-skins too, such as carp, which tend to shed their scales. The skin of all animals must be stripped of all flesh and fat. Then the skin is treated with chemicals and pinned flat to dry.

When the specimen is a large mammal like a lion, a model of its body is built up out of plaster on a foundation of steel and wood. Steel rods provide support for the limbs. If the skull of the animal is intact it is stripped of flesh and boiled to clean off the last vestiges of soft tissue. The actual skull is used to provide the framework for the head and face. A padding of wood wool is laid all over the foundation to give the soft effect of flesh. The skin is sewn onto the foundation and then the cosmetic work begins. The mouth and the tongue are modelled in plaster, painted with ordinary artist's oil paint and then varnished. The eye sockets are modelled in clay and painted, and then glass eyes are slotted into them. Different sizes and colours, of course, are needed for every species. Finally the mounted specimen is set up in a jungle of dried reeds, branches, and polystyrene rocks.

The best way to learn taxidermy is to start as a dedicated amateur, as Archie Henderson did:

'We have kids phoning every week wanting to learn the trade. But we've had to give up taking them on because they are mostly so hopeless. They think you're playing with animals. But just ask them to do something simple like skinning a foxhead, and they don't like it. You're messing around with brains and meat. It's not to everyone's taste.

There's a lot of variety. It's all seasonal. In the summer we have the trout and salmon. In the autumn we begin to pick up pike and people come in with pheasants. Skinning a fish—that's a tedious job. It takes about four hours; and you cut your hands to pieces on a pike—it has about seven hundred teeth, you know. Then it's got to be left to dry for three months; in the winter we have to heat the place all the time to dry the fish. Then it's painted and varnished. When it's skinned, a fish loses nearly all its colour, so we put on about seven layers of paint and varnish to get the effect back again.

You get satisfaction when you see people admiring your work in exhibitions. One nice thing about this job is that the things you do will still be here long after you are. They're saved.'

Saddler

There are three main points to look for in a well-made saddle: the stitching should be even and firm so that the saddle holds together and lasts for years; the saddle should make a snug fit on the horse's back; and it should look elegant, with graceful flowing lines.

Mick Martin is a master saddler with Giddens, the Royal saddlers. Until recently they used to have a quiet attic workshop just off New Oxford Street, which was an oasis of silence in the heart of London. But now the building has been demolished and the workshop has been moved to Islington.

Mick Martin works fast, selecting the right piece of leather from a huge pile, drawing a curving line on it and cutting along it with one motion of the saddler's semi-circular knife. Holding the leather between two large wooden pincers, the clamps, which are pushed together with his knees, he pierces holes with an awl, and sews with two needles and thread at once. He pushes them through the leather from either side, talking as he works:

'It takes me two and a half days to make a saddle. The old saddlers used to take a week. In most trades these days quality has deteriorated, but we have only slipped a little. For instance, they used to do twelve stitches to the inch, while we only do eight.

If a saddle doesn't fit it will take you hours to alter it—so it's worth getting it right first time. A couple of minutes spent here will save you hours later on. That's the main thing about this trade—pay attention to detail. The apprentices often start off by being smart-alecs. They try to cut corners and save time. I just smile and think that I went through it all years ago.'

A saddle is built up around a wooden framework called the tree. The tree is normally moulded out of laminated beechwood, and different shapes and weights of trees are made for the various types of saddles used for hunting, racing and show jumping. The seat of a saddle is normally made from the best quality pigskin, and the rest of the saddle may be of cowhide. The panels are stuffed and quilted, and care is taken not to stretch and strain the leather, thereby creating ugly bulges. All the time the craftsman has to be conscious of the line of the saddle that he is making:

'You've got to be a bit of an artist in this trade. You have to know exactly what you're doing before you do it. You have to recognize a line and a curve that's good. You can go some of the way with a ruler and pattern, but after that point you're on your own.

I can tell a saddle I made from about twenty paces. Every saddler has his own style. But the people you teach take after you. I might have to go a little nearer to recognize a saddle by someone I taught.

I'm in it for the money. You can earn £70 a week making saddles. The best incentive to a craftsman is the money. The government ought to realize that and they should help the trades.

There is a crackpot training scheme for this trade. They try to be too sophisticated. They teach the apprentices veterinary work, the anatomy of the horse, and they even tell them how to tell a good 'un. And the lads come out after eighteen months knowing nothing. They should concentrate on one thing: teach a lad just to be a saddler or a bridlemaker. When you've got a good saddler, pay him to take an apprentice.

My tools used to belong to my great-uncle. He left them to me in his Will, but I wasn't to have them until I finished my apprenticeship. You can't buy good saddling tools. They get passed down from one generation of saddlers to the next. It's a bit morbid, I know, but you have to wait for somebody to die before you get your tools.

One thing I like about this trade is that you're on your own. There is a tranquillity here. The world out there does not exist. And you can come to the end of the day, lean back and say, "That was a good day." Not like in an office where the "in" tray is empty and the "out" tray is full. There doesn't seem to be any satisfaction in that.'

According to the census figures there were 4,179 saddlers working in London in 1901. Now there may be only a handful of saddlers left, but they are enjoying a boom. English saddles are noted as the best in the world, and the London firms do a brisk export trade. Giddens themselves enjoyed a spectacular success recently: at a trade fair in the Middle East a customer came along and bought up their whole stock within minutes of the opening.

Racing Boat Builder

There was a time when boat-builders would not allow an outsider to see them at work for fear that the secrets of their methods would leak out to their competitors. They are more open now but each maker still has his own personal way of doing things. There are no written rules on how to make a boat. Each boat-builder has his book of sizes, but inevitably he adapts his measurements to fit in with the crew that he is building for.

The rowing fraternity are purists. They like their boats to be fitted for them like a pair of shoes. Every generation of rowing men has different ideas about the shape and weight of the boat that they want. So the best boat-builders are those who are flexible enough to accept the new ideas of their clients, and experienced enough to put these ideas into practice.

The firm of George Sims and Sons is a long-established institution on the Putney Embankment. The last of the Sims family retired in 1958 and now the firm is run by two young boat-builders. They work side by side on separate boats. A racing eight (for an eight-man crew) takes one man about six weeks to build; a four takes a month; and a single-man scull takes three weeks. Prices start at £420 for a scull. The order book is full up for about a year ahead. Customers range from local rowing clubs on the Thames to crews from Holland and southern Ireland.

The line of a boat is governed by the carved pieces of wood that form the foundation for the bows and the stern. Here beauty and function are the same thing. A graceful line will also be a streamlined and therefore a successful one. No amount of measuring will make a good line—it has to be judged by eye.

The foundation of a boat is a skeleton of ribs; spruce is the preferred wood. The shapes of the ribs are drawn out with templates, and then cut by hand and glued into place. It is important that all the ribs of the boat should be lined up together, and that the line they make is an evenly curving one. To test the line, the craftsman attaches a string to the stem of the boat, stretches it over the ribs and peers along it. If one of the ribs stands out from the others it has to be shaved down. When he is satisfied that he has the foundation for a graceful and speedy boat, he lays the 'skin' of thin plywood in sections over the ribs, and screws it into place with brass screws. Now the surface has to be sanded absolutely smooth, before several coats of varnish are applied—to ensure that the boat makes the least possible resistance in the water.

The arrangements of the seats in the boat are varied according to the height and weight of the men who are going to row in her. Joe Cunnah talks about his clients:

'In the old days the boats used to be made for an average height of man. But now they try to choose the crews all the same height. If you look at photographs of those crack East German crews, you see that the line of their heads is absolutely straight. That's more efficient, because if the crew are all the same height, the length of their stroke will be the same.

They all come to us with their theories. Nowadays we do what the client asks. We used to argue, but now we don't. They say what they want and we do it. They say that it's the boat that wins the race, but to my way of thinking it's the man who wins or loses. They ask us to take the fin off a boat—well, if we did that, they wouldn't be able to steer it. They ask us to make it much lighter; we do that, but the more you cut it down, the weaker it gets.

There are racing boats made of aluminium and fibreglass now. I think they will improve them, but to me the boats look dead in the water compared with a wooden boat; the wooden boat has got spring and movement in it. Fibreglass seems to suit sailing boats in a way that it doesn't suit racing boats yet. Maybe it'll come, but the market's limited. They might be able to turn out a boat every week, but very soon the market will be saturated. That's what keeps the small firms like us going; when the market's limited, the big firms keep out.'

The boat-building business is a pretty steady one, because the clubs that can afford it come back every two or three years for a new boat. Nevertheless, a boat that is well maintained will last for thirty years or more. One scull boat came back to the Sims firm for repair after forty-seven years of use.

Tennis Racket Stringer

John Duffield served his apprenticeship as a tennis racket maker, but he specializes in stringing, rather than frame-making. He can always recognize a racket that he has strung himself because he is one of the only stringers who still puts on the little extra embellishments that are a tradition of his trade. The thin red strings, known as 'trebling', at the bottom of a racket are decorative, but many stringers use only one string or drop them altogether. John Duffield still uses the full complement of three, and his own trade mark is a little bow of gut in the middle line of the trebling. 'Everyone says I'm a mug to pay attention to detail, but I like to do it.'

Mr Duffield's customers appreciate his attention to detail and he gets so much work that his average working day lasts from 7.30 a.m. to 9.0 at night. He comes to work at most weekends too. Most of his customers have been coming back for years and he does not have the heart to turn them away.

His career spans half a century that has seen a revolution in the tennis racket industry. When he finished his apprenticeship in 1920 racket frames were made of solid ash wood and carved by hand. Today they are mostly machine-made, from laminated wood.

> We used to do everything by hand in those days; we would pull the wood down with a draw knife and plane it with a rounded plane. My first governor was one of the old sort. Really tough. At the end of the week we would have made about three dozen frames and the last job was sanding them down. My God, how we sanded those frames. We sanded them until our faces were white with the dust. We sanded them until they were perfect. At the end of the job we used to have to take the whole batch down to the governor to be checked. He didn't just sample the batch. He looked at each in turn. He would take them in his hands and feel around them with his fingers. He turned them over and he'd look at every detail to see if they were finished off properly. Then he'd hand them all back to us: "Do 'em again," he'd say.

> We had to make the racket accurate to a quarter of an ounce. We used to test them all the time for balance, resting them on the finger. That's what makes a good racket, the balance of the thing. Well, nowadays you've only got the three different weights—heavy, medium and light. Just look at this racket; it was made too heavy so they hollowed out the handle and rammed cork in. To hell goes the balance, but they've got the weight right that way.

There is a machine that can do most of the work of stringing a racket, but Mr Duffield does not think much of it: 'I bought a stringing machine a few years back. But it was too slow, I couldn't afford to work at that speed.'

He takes a little under half an hour to string a racket. He cuts out the old strings, sands down the frame and cleans it with methylated spirit. He chooses a couple of coils of genuine sheep gut, one for the vertical strings and one for the horizontal. 'I always use English gut; it's the best in the world. You don't get much gut out of a sheep—just enough for one racket, that's all. The poor quality material is used for sausage casings. That's affected the gut trade too, you know. There are more sausages being eaten, so there's less gut available for this.'

Mr Duffield threads the gut into the first hole and ties it in with a double knot. (A small detail: most makers use a single knot, and sooner or later the knot works itself loose and the strings untie.) He threads the gut in and out of the holes of the racket at an astonishing speed, twisting the gut slightly to prevent it from unravelling. Now comes the most difficult job, tightening the strings to give the correct tension. He starts at the middle of the racket, tightening one string, drawing in the slack with the following string, and working outwards. He pulls with a force of 70 pounds, and the tension on the frame from one set of strings is so great that the frame would buckle if he did not support it with a steel cross-bar. When the other set of strings is in place there is an even tension all round the frame, and a support is not necessary. Mr Duffield tests the strings by plucking them like a guitar; he knows by the sound when they are at the right tension.

Mr Duffield has one of the few surviving one-man businesses in a trade where one or two large firms have cornered the market. This is how it happened:

'In about 1915, all the schools started taking up tennis. They all wanted junior rackets. Suddenly there was this terrific demand. So all the little firms—there were dozens of them then—started making junior rackets, and things were looking up. Then suddenly, for no reason at all, this large company decided to go into the sports trade. The word went round the trade that they were looking for makers and stringers, and they were offering a couple of shillings more than the other firms. As soon as they had got going they began to advertise. My God, they advertised. It was so successful that every kid in London wanted one of their junior rackets. The shops couldn't get enough of them—and they sold them for 4/- less than we could make them for. So for three or four years they made a big loss on the rackets, but they could cover it with profits on other things. And in that time they put nearly all the other small firms out of business. There was no sentiment with them.

One day my governor came to me and he said, "You know, John, I think we're going to have to pack up. I hope you'll be able to get fixed up somewhere." That's the way it was in those days. I had been with the firm thirty-five years, and there was not so much as an ounce of tobacco at the end of it.'

Mr Duffield tells this without a trace of bitterness. It is hard to imagine a man less interested in the commercial side of his trade:

'I'm keeping out of the rat-race; I've got no commitments. I charge everybody who comes in here the same as I would charge the shops wholesale. All the shops

I work for put another 100 per cent on to what I charge. It's all youngsters there—they've got the brains and we do the work. But there's one thing. I'm not sure about—where are they going to get the workers in years to come?

I did once try to get some youngsters interested in the trade. They sent up a couple of lads who had O-levels and A-levels. They all want the perks, pension schemes and a month's paid holiday and all that. What they want is posh multi-storey office blocks. They don't want to make things with their hands.'

Not many people have the peace of mind in an office block that Mr Duffield has found in his one-room workshop. 'I like it here. I would actually say that I prefer being here to being at home. I just go home to sleep. I haven't got anyone to go home to. I shall carry on here for as long as I can carry on. To die at the bench would suit me.'

CRAFT COMMITTEES, GUILDS AND SOCIETIES IN LONDON

Crafts Advisory Committee
12 Waterloo Place, London SW1 (01 838 8000)

Established in 1971 to promote the interests of artist-craftsmen and to channel Government funds into the crafts. Gives grants to crafts organizations and individuals. Aid to individual craftsmen includes loans and bursaries, workshop training schemes and financial help towards exhibitions, publications and films. The CAC also promotes craftsmen by exhibitions at the gallery in Waterloo Place, and publishes the bi-monthly magazine *Crafts*. Artist-craftsmen may apply to be included on the Index of Craftsmen, which is a register, available to the public, of artist-craftsmen examined and recommended by the CAC.

Federation of British Craft Societies
80A Southampton Row, London WC1 (01 242 2209)

A central secretariat for craft societies, providing many diverse organizations with a common voice. The many societies that make up the Federation include The Embroiderers' Guild, Designer Bookbinders, Craftsmen Potters Association of Great Britain, Guild of Glass Engravers and the Society of Designer Craftsmen. The Federation disseminates information among the member societies, publishes a newsletter and arranges discussion meetings.

British Crafts Centre
43 Earlham Street, London WC2 (01 836 6993)

Exhibits and sells work by contemporary artist-craftsmen at the spacious gallery in Earlham Street and also at the Craft Shop at the Victoria and Albert Museum. Provides an educational service for schools and colleges. Financed by membership subscriptions and by a grant from the Crafts Advisory Committee.

CoSIRA (Council for Small Industries in Rural Areas)
35 Camp Road, Wimbledon Common, London SW19 (01 947 6761)

A Government advisory service, which, in spite of a London base, is exclusively concerned with craftsmen in rural areas. CoSIRA's aim is to encourage and support small industries in the countryside, to prevent further depopulation of rural areas. It provides loans and assistance for small craft businesses, and runs training schemes for traditional trades, including saddlery, wrought ironwork and furniture restoration.

City and Guilds of London Institute
76 Portland Place, London W1 (01 580 3050)

Set up by the City Corporation and the Livery Companies in 1878, but almost independent now, being financed largely by its income from examination fees. The Institute is the main examining body for the manual trades, and City and Guilds qualifications are recognized the world over. There are some five hundred City and Guilds examinations, covering over two hundred trades, from welding to bespoke tailoring.

The Worshipful Company of Goldsmiths of London
Goldsmiths' Hall, Foster Lane, London EC2 (01 606 8971)

One of the eighty-six Livery Companies of the City and fifth in order of precedence. Since its foundation in the twelfth century, the Goldsmiths' Company has maintained a very close control and influence over the gold and silversmithing trade. The Company is the oldest hallmarking authority in the United Kindom, and each year some seven million articles are stamped here with the mark of the leopard's head. The Goldsmiths' Company maintains the apprenticeship system in silversmithing and supports the trade with prizes and patronage.

The Art Workers' Guild
6 Queen Square, London WC1 (01 837 3474)

An aristocrat among craft societies, originating in the nineteeth century from the Arts and Crafts Movement: William Morris was one of the first Masters of the Guild. The membership includes sculptors and architects as well as practising craftsmen of many kinds. The fine premises in Queen Square are sometimes let to other craft societies for meetings and exhibitions.

Clerkenwell Green Association for Craftsmen
27 Old Street, London EC 1 (01 253 4143)

An energetic local Association of craftsmen and their supporters, set up in 1970 to promote the survival of Clerkenwell as one of London's main centres for the craft trades. The Association provides an information and education service, as well as helping craftsmen to find workshop space. The Association's ambition, as yet unfulfilled, is to convert a large warehouse into workshop space, and to manage this as a co-operative, in which skilled craftsmen will be sponsored to take on young apprentices.

134

A DIRECTORY OF LONDON CRAFTSMEN

This list is in no way complete. It would not be possible to record every one of the huge and rapidly changing numbers of craftsmen working in London today. This is necessarily a selection, and inclusion here is not a guarantee that a craftsman would be right for every job in his field. Many craftsmen are specialists and clients should satisfy themselves that a chosen craftsman would be suitable for a particular commission. Craftsmen welcome genuine inquiries from intending purchasers but do not usually invite correspondence or interruption for other matters.

The names of the craftsmen or firms featured in the text or appearing in the photographs are marked with an *. In a few cases craftsmen are mentioned in the text but not listed here: this means that since the interview they have ceased trading in London for one reason or another.

A more comprehensive list of artist-craftsmen, recommended by the Crafts Advisory Committee, in the fields of glass, ceramics, jewellery, textiles etc, can be seen in the Committee's booklet *Craftsmen of Quality*, obtainable from 12 Waterloo Place, London sw1.

METALWORKERS

Blacksmiths

* A. H. Benbow, Townley St se17
C. B. Carey, 11 Claylands, sw8
W. R. Jewiss, 150 Abbey St se1
Ernest Layton, 136 Culford Rd, n1
J. H. Porter, 11 Pembroke Mews, w8
Charles Lisney, Arch 647 Blount St, e14
G. Townsend, 20 Beardell St, se19
R. H. Honeysett, Besley St, sw16
Cayford, 219a Belsize Rd, nw6
E. J. Margrie, 493 Fulham Palace Rd, sw6
C. Pillow, 49a Boscombe Rd, w12
H. S. Rogers, 57 Sturgess Avenue, nw4
C. Suckling, Golders Green Rd, nw11
S. Williams, 156 Tottenham Lane, n8

Farriers

* J. Geddes, Chivalry Rd, sw11
T. Dale, 23 Grafton Rd, Worcester Park, Surrey
R. R. Skippon, 10 Fashoda Rd, Bromley, Kent

Edge-tool Makers

* H. L. Pound, 84 Bonnington Sq, sw8

Wire-workers

* A. Hunter, 33b Shacklewell Lane, e8

Coppersmiths

Smith & Matthews, 13 Praed Mews, w2
J. W. Harlow, 1a Oxford Rd Nth, w4
J. Brierley, 9 Westmoor St, se7
Chesbur, Arch 11, Almond Rd, se16

Locksmith

B. J. Stevenson, Borough High St, se1

Springmaker

A. & H. Springs, Newington Garden Rd, n1

PRECIOUS METALS

Gold-beater

* G. Whiley, Victoria Rd, Ruislip, Middlesex

Gold and Silver Wire Drawer

Benton & Johnson, 26 Marshalsea Rd, SE1

Badge, Medal and Insignia Makers

* Padgett & Braham, 110 Shacklewell Rd, N16
John Pinches, 1 St Luke's Av, SW4

Silversmiths

* Stuart Devlin, 5 Albemarle Way, EC1
* Wakeley & Wheeler, 110 Shacklewell Rd, N16
Meiling Gartrell, 91 Turnmill St, EC1
Gerald Benney, 36 Bear Lane, SE1
Anthony Elson, 29 Clerkenwell Rd, EC1
Leslie Durbin, 62 Rochester Pl, NW1
Michael Driver, 23 Ansdell St, W8
Michael Murray, 27 Old St, EC1
William Phipps, 74 Clerkenwell Rd, EC1
(*spoons*)
Tony Laws, 8 Garrick St, WC2

Engravers

* T. & A. Wise, 110 Shacklewell Rd, N16
G. M. Betser, 15a Grafton St, W1

Enamellers

* C. F. Barnes, 376 St John St, EC1
Kempson and Mauger, 143 Rosebery Ave, EC1
Anthony Pugh, 110 Old St, EC1
Wild & Silverman, 33a York Rise, NW5

Gilder (on silver)

Pairpoints, 110 Shacklewell Rd, N16

Jewellers

Sarah Aberdare, 1 St Peter's Sq, W6
Alan Craxford, 14 Rusham Rd, SW12
John Donald, 120 Cheapside, EC2
Cynthia Jenkins, 27 Old St, EC1
Catherine Mannheim, 23 Glebe Pl, SW3
David Thomas, 46 Old Church St, SW3
Mary Dean, 27 Old St, EC1

Brian Hubble, 3 Arlington Cottages, Sutton Lane, W4
Stephen Maer, 18 Yerbury Rd, N19
Carol Nevard, 52 Middle Lane, N8

Teapot-handle Makers

* J. Figgins, 110 Shacklewell Rd, N16
W. E. Marshall, 60 Clerkenwell Rd, EC1 (*Also silver repairs*)

Pewtersmith

Englefields, Reflection House, Cheshire St, E2

WOODWORKERS

Furniture Makers

* Richard la Trobe Bateman, 23 Ceylon Rd, W14
H. J. Hatfield, 42 St Michael's St, W2 (*restorers*)
Martin Grierson, 5 Dryden St, WC2

Chair Caner

* J. G. Parish, 21 Islington Park St, N1

Cabinet-makers

* H & W Woodworkers, 111 Mortimer Rd, N1 (*instrument cases*)
J. B. Stocks, 13 Crescent Pl, SW3
Sid Waxler, 74 Luke St, EC2
Davis & Lewis, L.C.C. Workshops, Long St, E2
C. R. Perry, 65 Camden Mews, NW1

Wood turners

J. Bailey, Galatix Ho, Dallington St, EC1
E. W. Clark, 3 Coronet St, N1
Nichols & Nichols, Unit 1/9, Long St, E2
L. R. Tibbs, Progress Works, Warburton St, E8
A. Williams, 69 County St, SE1

Woodcarvers

* David Shoolheifer, 19/20 Sunbury Workshops, Swanfield St, E2

Brian O'Donnell, 21 Roche Walk, Carshalton, Surrey

H. E. Hilliard, Block 3, 3 Long St, EC3

Roger Board, 273, Putney Bridge Rd, SW15 (*carved fireplaces*)

Carvers and Gilders

G. D. Warder, 14 Hanway Pl, W1

S. Tissano, 89 Lansdowne Rd, W11

W. M. Kirchstein, 1a Maryon Mews, NW3

C. A. Westbury, 87 Arnold Rd, N15

Marquetry Makers

*A. Dunn, 42 Fleetwood Rd, NW10

*Fisher, 65 Redchurch St, E2

M. D. Fisher, Unit 22, Sunbury Workshops, Swanfield St, E2 (*also brass inlay*)

N. Simpson, 7 Woodlands Grove, Isleworth, Middlesex (*inlaid boxes*)

French Polishers

*Ernest Crook, Garner & Marney, 111 Mortimer Rd, N1

D. Bernstein, 12 Cheshire St, E2

C. F. Kemble, 2 New North Pl, EC2

J. Mulholland, Unit A, Block 13, Long St, E2

E. W. Wood, 39a Camden Sq, NW1

H. Morris, 20 Ensign St, E1

F. M. North, Unit 1, 11 Long St, E2

Barrow Makers

*Ellen Keeley, 33 Neal St, WC2

E. Howard, 23 Wheler St, E1

Brushmakers

J. Hoolahan, 748 Enid St, SE16 (*specialist brooms*)

A. S. Handover, Angel Yd, Highgate High St, N6 (*artist*)

Basketmakers

Blind Employment factory, 252, Waterloo Rd, SE1

Harrington and Marsh, 90a Oldfield Rd, N16

Coopers

*Tom Wood, Young's Brewery, Wandsworth High St, SW18

T. Grain, Horn Lane, SE10

Kingston Cooperage, 45a Acre Rd, Kingston, Surrey

Allen, Skinner & Parr, 470 Cantrell Rd, E1

Hall & Ryan, Temple Mill Lane, E15

Novicks Cooperage, 398 Rhodeswell Rd, E14

Trinidad Cooperage, Arch 307, Trinidad St, E14

MUSICAL INSTRUMENT MAKERS

*Crabb, 158 Liverpool Rd, N1 (*concertinas*)

*Flutemakers' Guild, 110 Shacklewell Rd, N16 (*flutes*)

*Paxman, 116 Long Acre, WC2 (*horns*)

*Paul Voigt, 2 Gerrard Pl, W1 (*violin repairs*)

*Stephen Gottlieb, 27 Old St, EC1 (*lutes*)

*V. Chiappa, 31 Eyre St Hll, EC1 (*automatic organs*)

*A. Noterman, 111 Frithville Gardens, W12 (*organs*)

*John Broadwood, 1 Brunel Rd, W3 (*pianos*)

*Keith Harding, 93 Hornsey Rd, N7 (*musical boxes*)

Albert Cooper, 9 West Rd, SW4 (*flutes*)

T. V. Howarth, 31 Chiltern St, W1 (*oboes*)

Boosey & Hawkes, Deansbrook Rd, Edgware. (*Many types, chiefly brass*)

The Harpsichord Centre, 47 Chiltern St, W1 (*harpsichords*)

Edward Withers, 22 Wardour St, W1 (*violins, viols*)

Martin Bouette, 27 Old St, EC1 (*violins*)

W. Danemann, 6 Northampton St, N1 (*pianos*)

Robert Morley, 4 Belmont Hill, SE13 (*pianos, harpsichords*)

Mark Stevenson, 18 Gunter Grove, SW10 (*clavichords, spinets etc*)

J. & A. Beare, 179 Wardour St, W1 (*violin repairs*)

J. F. Pyne, 9 Leighton Pl, NW5 (*piano keys*)

N. P. Mander, St Peters Ave, E2 (*organs*)

Bishop & Son, 58 Beethoven St, W10 (*organs*)

Rose Morris, 32 Gordon House Rd, NW5 (*military band*)

Neil Hansford, 39 Pottery Lane, W11 (*medieval bowed instruments, spinets*)

Michael Sprake, 39a Pottery Lane, W11 (*lutes and baroque guitars*)

Brian Cohen, 37 Pottery Lane, W11 (*lutes*)

Maish Weisman, 37 Pottery Lane, W11 (*vihuela, lutes*)

A DIRECTORY OF LONDON CRAFTSMEN

BOOKS AND PRINTING

Vellum Maker

*H. Band, Brentway, Brentford, Middlesex

Calligraphy and Illumination

Donald Jackson, 28 Grove Lane, SE5
Madaleine Dinkel, 233 King St, W6 (*calligraphy*)
Heather Child, 188 Cromwell Rd, SW5

Hand-printed Books

Ann Brunskill, World's End Press, 64 Wapping High St, E1

Bookbinders

*W. T. Morrell, 4 Nottingham Court WC2
Sangorski & Sutcliffe, 1 Poland St, W1
Fiona Campbell, 158 Lambeth Rd, SE1 (*contemporary*)
Denise Lubett, 2 Oakwood Mansions, W14
Sally Lou Smith, 42a Camden High St, NW1 (*contemporary*)
E. Seabrook, 106 Gt Russell St, WC1

Edge-gilders

*G. H. Patmore, 8 Tilney Court, Old St EC1
F. Clark & T. Scott, 4 Nottingham Court WC2

Copperplate Engraver

*Stan Apsey, 91 Turnmill St EC1

Wood Engravers' Blockmaker

*T. N. Lawrence, 2/4 Bleeding Heart Yard, Greville St, EC1

Woodblock Printmaker

White Ink, 2 Shelford Pl, N16

Silkscreen Printmaker

*Christopher Prater, Kelpra Studios, 19 Bath St, EC1

Lithographic Printmakers

Curwen Press, 114 Tottenham Court Rd, W1
Petersburg Press, 14 Priory Ave, W4

Copperplate Printmakers

*Thomas Ross, 5 Manfred Rd, SW15
Hugh Stoneman, Islington Studio, 107 St Pauls Rd, N1

CLOTHES AND SUNDRIES

Hat Makers

*S. Patey, 15b Amelia St, SE17 (*all kinds of hard hats*)
H. C. Corne, 102 Evelina Rd, SE15 (*theatrical*)
A. & L. Corne, 154 Tooley St, EC1 (*military*)

Bespoke Tailors

* Gieves and Hawkes, 1 Savile Row, W1
Airey & Wheeler, 8 Sackville St, W1
W. Bill, 28 Old Bond St, W1
Blades, 8 Burlington Gardens, W1
H. Huntsman, 11 Savile Row, W1
Jones, Chalk & Dawson, 6 Sackville St, W1
Nutters, 35a Savile Row, W1
Henry Poole, 10 Cork St, W1
Pope & Bradley, 35 Sackville St, W1
Maxwell Vine, 7 Sackville St, W1
Sandon, 7/8 Savile Row, W1

Specialist Robemakers

Ede & Ravenscroft, 93 Chancery Lane, WC2 (*academic, legal robes, legal wigs*)
Thomas Pratt, 34 Southampton St, WC2 (*clerical tailors*)
Louis Grosse, 36 Manchester St, W1 (*Church vestments*)

Swordmakers

*Joseph Starkey, 19a Iliffe Yd, SE17
Wilkinson Swords, Brunel Rd, W3
Robert White, 25 Shelton St, WC2 (*theatrical*)

Swordstick Maker

* Mr Drew, James Smith & Son, 53 New Oxford Street, WC1

138

Shoemakers

* John Lobb, 9 St James's St, SW1
James Taylor, 4 Paddington St, W1
John Moss, 26 Camden Rd, NW1 (*orthopaedic*)

Shoe Lasts and Trees

S. Allen, 37 Gosfield St, W1
H. Peen, 21 Heard St, W1
and at the shoemakers (*above*)

Leather Goods

Algernon Asprey, 27 Bruton St, W1

Embroidery, Textiles, Weaving etc

Mary Ball, 22 Vanbrugh Hill, SE3 (*woven wall hangings*)
Lucy Goffin, 15 St Johns Wood Terrace, NW8 (*quilting, patchwork etc*)
Constance Howard, 43 Cambridge Rd Sth, W4 (*appliqué wallhangings*)
Lady Mary Strachey, 8 Pembroke Sq, W8 (*crochet*)
Joanna Buxton, 401½ Wandsworth Rd, SW8 (*woven tapestries*)
Peter & Marian Daglish, 13 Esmond Rd, W4 (*wallhangings in wool*)
Penelope Ephson, 401½ Wandsworth Rd, SW8
Alison Mitchell, 111 New Kings Rd, SW6 (*decorative weaving*)
Muswell Hill Weavers, 65 Rosebery Rd, N10 (*weavings*)
Fianne Bastick, 16 Drayson Mews, W8 (*fabric printing*)
Juliet Bloye, 43 Belgrave Rd, SW1 (*pictorial batik*)
Harriet Cameron, 3 Fielding Rd, W14 (*hand-painted silk*)
Olivia Brett, 7 Clarendon Cross, W11 (*batik window blinds*)
Mary Moore, 30 Baker St, W1 (*ecclesiastical: altar linens etc*)
Watts, 7 Tufton St, SW1 (*ecclesiastical: altar frontals etc*)
M. Hand, 25 Lexington St, W1 (*gold embroidery*)

Hand Knitting

Kaffe Fassett, 62 Fordwych Rd, NW2
Anne Fewlass, 27 Tabley Rd, N7
Esther Pearson, 51½ Stroud Green Rd, N4

Fancy Feather Trimmers

Louis Bund, 16 Ramillies St, W1

ENVIRONMENTAL CRAFTSMEN

Architectural Sculptors

* Kenneth Gardner, c/o Clerk of Works, St Pauls Cathedral, EC4
Bradfords, 61 Borough Rd, SE1 (*wood/stone carving etc*)

Stone Mason

J. Bysouth, Dorset Rd, N15

Model Maker

Nicholas Gaffney, Thorps Modelmakers, 98 Grays Inn Rd, WC1

Architectural Decorators

* G. Jackson, Rathbone Works, Rainville Rd, W6 (*composition enrichment, scagiola, fibrous plaster etc*)
M. Binnings, Bloomsbury Frame Works & Repairs, 62 Lambs Conduit St, WC1 (*composition work*)
J. G. McDonough, 347a New Kings Rd, SW6 (*fibrous plaster*)

Grainers & Marblers

T. E. Clarke, 32 Landman Hse, Galleywall Rd, SE16
Reginald Stocks, 64 Northchurch Rd, N1
F. H. Robson, 96 Elms Crescent, SW4
Ann Talbot, 19a Cromwell Rd, SW7 (*marbled furniture*)

Signpainters

Edmett, 43 Lambs Conduit St, WC1
F. G. Fowle, 260 Balham High Rd, SW17 (*showman decorator*)

Stained Glass Makers

* Goddard & Gibbs, 41/49 Kingsland Rd, E2

Luxford Stained Glass Studio, 83 East Barnet Rd, New Barnet, Herts
Brian Thomas, 3 Hill Rd, NW8
Carl Edwards, 11 Lettice St, SW6
Ray Bradley, 3 Orchard Studios, Brook Green W6

Candlemaker

* Michael Holt at Prices, Belmont Works, York Rd, Battersea

Carpet Makers

Robert Wallace, St John's Gardens, Benjamin St, EC1
David Hill, 11A Westwood Hill, SE26 (*woven wallhangings, rugs*)
Alison Mitchell, 26 King Henry's Rd, NW3 (*woven cushions, rugs etc*)

INSTRUMENTS, GLASS AND CERAMICS

Clockmakers

* George Daniels, c/o Sotheby's Ltd, 34 New Bond St, W1 (*pocket watches*)
* A. Lee, 122 St John St, EC1
A. Rowley & H. Parkes, 17 Briset St, EC1
William Andrewes, Enfield Hse, Windmill Hll, NW3

Clock Dial Painter

* E. C. Longcluse, 16 Clerkenwell Green, EC1

Barometer Makers

* Garner & Marney, 41 Southgate Rd, N1
O. Comitti, 51 Mt Pleasant, WC1
J. McCarthy, 40 Rosebery Ave, WC1

Camera Maker

* Louis Gandolfi, 2 Borland Rd, SE15

Glassmakers

* Whitefriars Glass, Tudor Rd, Wealdstone, Middlesex
The Glasshouse, 65 Long Acre, WC2
T. & W. Ide, Glasshouse Fields, E1

R. Wilkinson, 45 Wastdale Rd, SE23 (*cutting & restoration*)

Glass Engravers

* Alec Cobbe (moved to 16A Lyndewood Rd, Cambridge)
Stephen Rickard, The Old Vicarage, Vicarage Park, SE18
Simon Whistler, 5 Fullerton Rd, SW18

Ceramics

Mohammed Abdalla, 13 King Henry's Rd, NW3
Glenys Barton, 72 Brocklebank Rd, SW18
Kenneth Clark, 10a Dryden St, WC2 (*ceramic tiles*)
Emmanuel Cooper, 38 Chalcot Rd, NW1
Barry Guppy, 6 Moreton St, SW1
Anita Hoy, 50 Julian Av, W3
Jacqueline Poncelet, 145 Pancras Rd, NW1 (*bone china*)
John Ward, 65 Priolo Rd, SE7
Val Barry, 86 Cecile Park, N8
Tony Grant, 53 Southdean Gardens, SW19
Janice Tchalenko, 30 Therapia Rd, SE22

SPORTS AND GAMES

Gunsmiths

John Wilkes, 79 Beal St, W1
Thomas Bland, 21 New Row, WC2
Boss, 13 Cork St, W1
Churchill, 7 Bury St, SW1
James Purdey, 57 S. Audley St, W1
Bryant, 35 Astbury Rd, SE15 (*leather gun cases*)

Taxidermists

* London Taxidermist Studio, 182 Dalston Lane, E8
Rowland Ward, Crawley Rd, N22
Janson, 44 Gt Russell St, WC1 (*insect setting*)

Saddlers

* W. & H. Gidden, 20 Brunswick Pl, N1
George Parker, 12 Upper St Martin's Lane, WC2

Racing Boat Builders

* George Sims, The Embankment, sw15
E. Ayling, Embankment, sw15 (*oars*)
W. J. Colley, Lower Mall, w6
Edwin Phelps, The Embankment, sw15
P. R. Anderson, 140 Pennington St, e1 (*sail-makers*)

Miscellaneous Sports

* John Duffield, 11 Northington St, wc1 (*tennis rackets*)
Holbrows, 12 Upper St Martin's Lane, wc2 (*polo sticks*)
John Edgington, 47 Old Woolwich Rd, se10 (*flags*)
John Bennett, 157 Old Kent Rd, se1 (*billiards*)

Toys

John Wright, 14 Dagmar Passage, n1 (*carved marionettes*)

BIBLIOGRAPHY

Alexander, Bruce. *Crafts and Craftsmen.* Croom Helm, 1974
Anon. *A General Description of All Trades.* 1774
Anon. *The Book of English Trades.* 1824
Arnold, J. *The Shell Book of Country Crafts.* John Baker, 1968
Bates, Kenneth, F. *Enamelling, Principles and Practice.* Funk and Wagnalls, 1974
Booth, Charles. *Life and Labour of London.* Williams and Norgate, 1889
Burdett, Eric. *The Craft of Bookbinding.* David and Charles, 1975
Casson, Michael. *The Craft of the Potter.* BBC Publications 1977
Child, Peter. *The Craftsman Woodturner.* G. Bell, 1977
CoSIRA. *Craft Workshops in the Countryside, England and Wales.* Published annually.
Crafts Advisory Committee. *Craftsmen of Quality.* 1976.
Dobbs, Brian. *The Last Shall be First.* Elm Tree Books, 1972.
Edwards, E. H. *Saddlery.* J. A. Allen, 1971.
Gilding, Bob. *The Journeyman Coopers of East London: Workers' Control in an Old London Trade.* Ruskin College History Workshop, 1971.
Hasluck, Paul. *Glass Writing, Embossing and Fascia Work.* Cassell, 1906
Hasluck, Paul. *Practical Graining and Marbling.* Cassell, 1902
Hasluck, Paul. *Saddle and Harness Making.* Cassell, 1904
Hawkins, J. H. *History of the Worshipful Company of the Art or Mistery of Feltmakers of London.* 1917
Heron-Allen, E. *Violin Making As It Was and Is.* 1947
Hughes, Graham. *Modern Silver.* Studio Vista, 1967
H.M.S.O. *Dictionary of Occupational Terms.* 1927
Kilby, Kenneth. *The Cooper and His Trade.* John Baker, 1971
Leach, Bernard. *A Potter's Book.* Faber, 1969
Leach, Bernard. *The Potter's Challenge.* Souvenir Press, 1976
Lincoln, William A. *The Art and Practice of Marquetry.* Thames and Hudson, 1971
Long, Marilyn. *Covent Garden and Her Craftsmen.* 1975
Lucie-Smith, Edward: *The World of the Makers.* Paddington Press, 1975
Middleton, Bernard. *A History of Craft Bookbinding Techniques.* Hafner, 1963
Oughton, Frederick. *The History and Practice of Woodcarving.* Stobart, 1976
Parry, John P. *Graining and Marbling.* Crosby Lockwood, 1957
Parsons, Denys. *What's Where in London.* BP, 1972
Pooley, Ernest. *The Guilds of the City of London.* Collins, 1945
Rees, J. Aubrey. *The English Tradition.* Muller, 1934
Reyntiens, Patrick. *The Technique of Stained Glass.* Batsford, 1967
Robson, Leonard C. F. *The Farriers of London.* 1949
Salaman, R. A. *A Dictionary of Tools Used in the Woodworking and Allied Trades 1700-1970.* Allen and Unwin, 1975
Singer, Charles, *et al. A History of Technology.* OUP, 1954-8
Smith, Philip, *New Directions in Bookbinding.* Studio Vista, 1975
Tomlinson, Charles. *The Useful Arts and Manufactures of Great Britain.* 1860
Turner, Ralph. *Contemporary Jewelry.* Studio Vista, 1976
Wainwright, David. *The Piano Makers.* 1975
Whistler, Laurence. *The Image on the Glass.* John Murray, 1976
Wilson, Aubrey. *London's Industrial Heritage.* David and Charles, 1967
Wymer, Norman. *English Town Crafts.* 1949